FEAR OF CRIME

SUNY Series in New Directions in Crime and Justice Studies
Austin T. Turk, Editor

FEAR OF CRIME

Interpreting Victimization Risk

Kenneth F. Ferraro

STATE UNIVERSITY
OF NEW YORK
PRESS

One section of chapter 2 draws on Randy L. LaGrange, Kenneth F. Ferraro, and Michael Supancic, 1992, "Perceived Risk and Fear of Crime: Role of Social and Physical Incivilities," *Journal of Research in Crime and Delinquency* 29:311–334. Portions of chapter 3 appear in slightly different form in either: Kenneth F. Ferraro and Randy LaGrange, 1987, "The Measurement of Fear of Crime," *Sociological Inquiry* 57:70–101 or Kenneth F. Ferraro and Randy L. LaGrange, 1988, "Are Older People Afraid of Crime?" *Journal of Aging Studies* 2:277–287. Portions of chapters 3 and 6 appear in slightly different form in Kenneth F. Ferraro and Randy L. LaGrange, 1992, "Are Older People Most Afraid of Crime? Reexamining Age Differences in Fear of Victimization," *Journal of Gerontology: Social Sciences* 47:S233–244. Portions of chapter 7 appear in slightly different form in Kenneth F. Ferraro, "Women's Fear of Crime: Sexual and Nonsexual Victimization," paper presented at the annual meeting of the 1995 North Central Sociological Association.

Published by
State University of New York Press, Albany

© 1995   State University of New York

Production by Susan Geraghty
Marketing by Fran Keneston

Printed in the United States of America

For information, address State University of New York Press,
State University Plaza, Albany, N.Y., 12246

Library of Congress Cataloging-in-Publication Data

Ferraro, Kenneth F.
      Fear of crime : interpreting victimization risk /Kenneth F.
Ferraro
            p.   cm.—(SUNY series in new directions in crime and justice
studies)
            Includes bibliographical references and indexes.
            ISBN 0-7914-2369-7 (alk. paper).—ISBN 0-7914-2370-0 (pbk. :
acid-free)
            1. Fear of crime — United States.   2. Victims of crimes — United
States — Psychology.   I. Title. II. Series: SUNY series in new directions in criminal
justice studies.
      HV6791.F47 1995
      362.88'01'9—dc20   94-10628
                                                                                                    CIP

10 9 8 7 6 5 4 3 2 1

To John F. Ferraro and
Patrick J. Welsh

CONTENTS

LIST OF FIGURES

LIST OF TABLES

PREFACE

This book is the result of a ten-year research odyssey examining the phenomenon of fear of crime. While reading the scholarly literature on fear of crime during the early 1980s, I was struck by the findings which identified older people as the age group most fearful in American society and began to critically analyze the literature. I invited Randy LaGrange, a criminologist, to join me in this venture of critiquing previous research. We identified several problems with how fear of crime was defined and measured and went into print suggesting how to improve upon the literature (Ferraro and LaGrange 1987, 1988; LaGrange and Ferraro 1987). We take some encouragement in playing a role—spearheaded by Mark Warr—in actually changing the way people research the subject. This is evident in recent changes in the measures of fear of crime used in the British Crime Survey and the National Crime Survey as well as in other investigations.

Professor LaGrange took the next initiative in collecting some pilot data which put into practice our proposals for measuring fear of crime. That pilot survey of one county in North Carolina provided findings which questioned the "axiom" that older people are most afraid of crime but replicated some of the other findings (LaGrange and Ferraro 1989). To uncover an empirical reality which we hypothesized to exist was indeed exciting; so, with help from the AARP Andrus Foundation, we collected data from a national sample to verify and extend our findings (Ferraro and LaGrange 1992; LaGrange, Ferraro, and Supancic 1992).

This book draws extensively from that national sample and from other data sources to develop and test a risk interpretation model of fear of crime. Fear of crime is defined as an emotional reaction of dread or anxiety to crime or symbols that a person associates with crime. Thus, it would seem logical that a person's judgments about the crime risk would be salient in models and theories regarding the scientific study of fear of crime. Yet, I was surprised that most previous research did not explicitly consider the influence of risk or perceived risk of crime on fear. In the study described here, I examine the influence of both objective or "official" risk and perceived risk on fear of crime. The model presented here develops the theoretical rationale for viewing perceived risk as *the* pivotal factor influencing fear of crime. Envisioned in the model is a process whereby people interpret ecological information regarding crime and victimization to judge their risk of specific victimizations. Once this judgment is made, two outcomes are most likely: (a) people may modify their behavior or environment to minimize high risk and/or (b) they may become afraid.

The present study is unique for using concepts and variables from macro- and micro-levels of sociological analysis in an integrated framework for studying the subject. Moreover, it is the first study to do this with national data from the United States. All of the analyses, while extending my previous work, are fresh; this is the first time that I have integrated measures of "official" or objective risk while trying to explain fear of crime. The findings are especially relevant to the United States, but the process of interpreting risks is not confined by national boundaries; indeed, I welcome scholars from other countries to attempt to replicate, or refute, the findings presented here.

The book does not chronicle the research odyssey but concentrates on the theoretical model and findings which result from the most recent work—the integration of "official" risk. For instance, the findings show that adult perceptions of victimization risk generally correlate with official crime statistics and that fear is strongly shaped by perceived risk. Contrary to considerable previous research, older people are *not* the age group which manifests the highest levels of fear of victimization. Indeed, the higher fear of crime found among younger respondents correlates well with victimization risk and questions the existence of the "victimization/fear paradox" by age. Women of all ages express higher levels of fear largely due to the "shadow of sexual assault" (i.e., women's perception of the contingency of sexual assault coupled with most types of crime). The findings and the process of reaching them has enriched my understanding of how people interpret and make sense of their everyday world.

ACKNOWLEDGMENTS

Since inviting Randy LaGrange to join my research program on fear of crime, I have found him to be a superb collaborator and colleague. Whereas fear of crime is one of the two major research programs I pursue, I especially enjoyed having Randy as a "partner *on* crime." He was invited to join me as a co-author of this book but declined to do so, largely for personal reasons and other obligations. In his humble demeanor, he probably would not claim much influence over this work. Yet, his mark is clearly present, and I thank him for carefully reading the entire work.

Another colleague who has helped where Randy left off is John Stahura. His grasp of criminology and the ecological determinants of crime have been especially helpful for me to probe micro/macro linkages. His comments on the manuscript and answers to my numerous queries are deeply appreciated.

Other colleagues whose comments and assistance in one way or another I gratefully acknowledge include Ronald Akers, Elizabeth Grauerholz, Charles F. Longino, Jr., JoAnn Miller, Robert Perrucci, Julian Roebuck, Jack W. Spencer, Cathy Streifel, Mark Warr, and Fredric Wolinsky. I also appreciate the helpful comments from anonymous reviewers selected by the State University of New York Press.

On the institutional front, several organizations provided indispensable help. First, the AARP Andrus Foundation supported the research project to collect the survey data used here. I appreciate the help of Drs. Kenneth Cook, Pamela Kerin, and Betsy Sprouse in supporting the research project and the dissemination of the results.

Second, Purdue University has been good to me in a number of ways. Pertinent to this project, a one-semester fellowship with the School of Liberal Arts' Center for Social and Behavioral Sciences released me from teaching duties to concentrate on this book. I am especially grateful to Dean David Caputo and Robert Browning, Brant Burleson, Clark Larsen, Joan Duda, Dean Knudsen, Stuart Offenbach, and Rachel Stark. I thank Janet Neel for her superb work on all the graphic presentations herein. I benefitted greatly from Donita Ames's help with library and technical assistance as well as clerical support from Evelyn Douthit and Barb Puetz.

Third, the survey data were collected while I was on the sociology faculty of Northern Illinois University. I was very pleased with the quality of data collected by Northern's Public Opinion Laboratory. It was a delight to work with William McCready who went beyond the call of duty in assisting instrumentation and pretesting.

Finally, the data on crime rates in the U.S. were made available in part by the Inter-University Consortium for Political and Social Research. These data are actually from the *Uniform Crime Reports*, collected under the auspices of the U.S. Department of Justice, Federal Bureau of Investigation. None of the people or organizations mentioned here bears any responsibility for the analyses or interpretations presented.

When it comes to socio-emotional help, no one does more or better than my lovely wife, Linda. A lifetime is not too long to live as friends. Next in line are Charisse, Nathan, and Justin who help me to refocus on the important things in life. Remember the Strong Tower.

CHAPTER 1

Whither Fear of Crime?

Crime is normal because a society exempt from it is utterly impossible.

Emile Durkheim

Scarcely a day passes that we are not hit anew with penetrating stories of criminal victimization. A thirteen-year-old girl shoots a cab driver in the back of the head, killing him, to avoid paying a six-dollar fare. A van carrying Hasidic Jews home from a hospital visit is sprayed with bullets. Drive-by shootings repeatedly occur in major cities. Scandals of fraud, embezzlement, and "impropriety" appear almost commonplace. Print and electronic media present frank depictions of violence and property crime, which show that America is under a siege of criminal activity. Indeed, the popularity of television means that most Americans can often watch criminal events or police reactions to them in living color— sometimes live. The preponderance of crime-related television shows and the preponderance of news stories devoted to crime are evidence that Americans spend considerable time pondering criminal victimization and efforts to constrain or punish offenders.

Yet what do we know about how most people really think about crime? While the media regularly reveals heinous acts of crime, terrorism, and incivility throughout the nation, does this shower of "crime news" make much difference in terms of daily living? Do violent crimes in New York City or Los Angeles make a difference to those who live in the respective suburbs, or even in Peoria? Are people aware of the relative risks of various types of crime and how that risk varies by communities? Are they afraid of crime? And, if so, how afraid are they? How do people interpret their own victimization risks in the course of everyday living? Do perceived crime risks and fears follow ecological patterns similar to those for crime? Who is most likely to be accurate in judging crime risk in their communities? Who is most likely to be afraid?

1

And do all these interpretive processes make any difference in daily behavior to avoid or protect oneself from crime? These and related questions are the focus of this book.

This is an empirical study of how people interpret criminal realities and victimization potentials around them. The social consequences of crime extend beyond those who are directly victimized, and this research focuses on one such consequence: fear. It is not intended to give directions on reducing fear of crime but may identify interpretive processes which can be seen as plausible intervention avenues. In a more general sense, the book goes beyond risk and fear of crime to examine how people interpret and make sense of their world. Using criminal victimization as the case in point, the conceptual framework and model developed may be fairly easily adapted to explain other phenomena from health behavior to decision-making processes.

While there is a clear consensus that crime is a serious social problem in the United States, there are two areas of controversy regarding reactions to it which are germane to this research. The first concerns the distribution and etiology of perceived risk and fear. Some scholars and policymakers paint a picture of rampant fear of crime in America, especially among older people, in part due to a *mis*understanding of true risk (e.g., Clemente and Kleiman 1976; National Institute of Justice 1992; Ollenburger 1981). On the other hand, some researchers show that fear of crime exists in America but that it is closely related to risk and not nearly as pervasive a social problem as some suggest (Warr 1984; Yin 1982). Although it may be impossible to convince some that the findings from this project can settle the controversy, the present investigation represents the first national study to examine the relationship between crime risk and fear among various age groups. In addition, the most recent developments in survey research for the measurement of fear of crime are applied. Survey data on perceived risk and fear of crime are linked to official statistics to examine the accuracy of public awareness of crime risk and emotional reactions to it manifested in fear.

The second controversy hinges on strategies to overcome fear of crime. While this is not the focus of this investigation, it may be useful to consider the policy significance of this research. Regardless of the prevalence of fear of crime in modern societies, some effort is needed to reduce it. Edward Kennedy (1972) argued over two decades ago in a Senate hearing on housing for older people that "A decent and safe living environment is an inherent right of all elderly citizens." No one disagrees with the goals of creating safe communities and reducing fear of crime but *how* to achieve these goals is hotly debated. The issue of contention remains the object for change.

The traditional and most widely accepted premise for reducing fear of crime has hinged on the formidable task of reducing crime. Yet, a more recent position, what some writers refer to as *perceptual criminology*, has arisen with the realization that many of the problems associated with crime, including fear, are independent of actual victimization. Crime is often viewed as a social problem, whether or not a person (or the person's significant others) has actually been recently victimized, because it may lead to decreased social integration, out-migration, restriction of activities, added security costs, and avoidance behaviors.[1] As Warr (1985) states: "And like criminal victimization itself, the consequences of fear are real, measurable, and potentially severe, both at an individual and social level" (p. 238).

Because people may be concerned about or afraid of crime without experiencing victimization, some scholars have argued that more than just crime should be targeted for change. Indeed, some scholars go so far as to conclude that fear of crime is a more severe problem than crime itself (Clemente and Kleiman 1976). Accepting this premise can lead to a host of strategies to affect public beliefs about crime. For example, consider the concept of *symbolic reassurance* offered by Henig and Maxfield (1978) which includes increasing police visibility and community interaction in order to change public beliefs about crime. Few may argue with initiatives to change public beliefs about crime in order to limit reactions such as out-migration and fear. The tension among scholars and policymakers arises, however, when changing public beliefs is seen as a substitute for or more important than reducing criminal victimization per se. In other words, if a zero-sum game is played, how much effort should be given to the two objectives? Of course, the other important questions surrounding this debate are whether public beliefs about crime are inaccurate, irrational, or even in need of change. The interrelatedness of the basic science questions on the distribution and etiology of crime risk and fear and the policy questions on appropriate intervention avenues should now be readily apparent. If our answers to the first question are in error or ill-informed, then we will invest in social interventions for the wrong people or under the wrong circumstances. As a result, it is possible that such interventions could actually create fear of crime rather than reduce it—an iatrogenic effect.

Many published reports contend that the public beliefs about crime are inaccurate, largely because of media distortion in covering crime (Baker, Nienstedt, Everett, and McCleary 1983). Quinney's (1970) comments on the distortion of criminal realities by the media were seminal in this regard: "Coverage of crime by the mass media, therefore, is not only selective but is a distortion of the everyday world of crime" (p. 284). The distortion is often attributed to the "overemphasis on violent crime, the creation of artificial crime waves, the use of crime news as 'filler,' misleading reports of crime statistics, and police control of crime news" (Warr 1982, p. 187).

While media no doubt play a significant role in shaping perceived risk and fear of crime, other factors may influence such beliefs. Moreover, there are comparatively few studies which make direct tests of public beliefs about crime in relation to objective data. What few studies offer direct tests of public beliefs suggest that the media distortion thesis may be an oversimplification. Generally speaking, the studies reflect an overall pattern of considerable public accuracy in estimating crime risk (Kleinman and David 1973; Lewis and Salem 1986; McPherson 1978; Stafford and Galle 1984; Warr 1980, 1982) although certain social categories and ethnic groups appear more accurate than others in judging the prevalence of crime (Janson and Ryder 1983). Each of the aforementioned studies is limited by studying the relationship between objective and perceived risk of crime among only one urban place or perhaps a limited sample of metropolitan areas. The present study seeks to extend our knowledge by using national data including urban and rural areas.

In short, the central research question focuses on the distribution and etiology of fear of crime in America. I seek to identify those persons who are most afraid of crime and offer explanations for their fear. Fear of crime is an emotional response of dread or anxiety to crime or symbols that a person associates with crime (Ferraro and LaGrange 1987, 1992). To produce a fear reaction in humans, a recognition of a situation as possessing at least potential danger, real or imagined, is necessary. This conception of potential danger is what we may call perceived risk and is clearly defined by the actor in association with others. Therefore, although many previous studies of fear of crime do not explicitly consider the concept of risk or perceived risk in the modeling process, the approach taken here is to consider perceived risk as central to the entire interpretive process.

In the process of answering the general questions about who is most afraid of crime and why, we can also address a series of specific research questions raised by previous researchers regarding age and gender differences in fear of crime. The findings of this study have considerable policy relevance as we try to tame the crime monster in American society—but the emphasis here is on improving our understanding of what produces fear of crime, not advocating selective intervention efforts. I see fear of crime influenced by knowledge and experience of criminal realities, environmental context, and biographical features. In order to reach the stated objectives, our first step is to articulate the theoretical approach to be used in studying it.

CHAPTER 2

Interpreting Criminal Realities: "Risky Business"

As in all sciences, in sociology interpretation is all.

Philip Rieff

Research on fear of crime has drawn considerable attention over the last two decades as researchers have attempted to identify why certain social categories reportedly have such high levels of fear. The bulk of this research has focused on how status characteristics such as sex and age affect fear of crime, and much of the research lacks a clear theoretical framework. Rather, the emphasis has been upon locating fear of crime among the populace and providing insight into why people in certain social categories are fearful. Another recent criticism of this literature which merits detailed consideration is the omission of risk and/or perceived risk from models of how people interpret potential victimization. As the following analysis suggests, perhaps the omission of risk from previous studies and the lack of clearly articulated theoretical approaches are related.

Despite the logic of considering perceived risk as a predictor of fear of crime and the implicit discussion of risk in the literature, numerous studies on fear of crime do not directly measure either risk or perceived risk of crime (e.g., Liska, Sanchirico, and Reed 1988).[1] Yet, in all of the studies that considered risk or perceived risk of crime, it played an important role in explaining fear of crime (e.g., Ferraro and LaGrange 1992).[2] Therefore, it would seem that any scientific approach to the subject of fear of crime should give explicit attention to risk interpretation processes. Although the approach taken here emphasizes symbolic interaction theory, additional theoretical perspectives are integrated to develop the risk interpretation approach. In this chapter, I begin by reviewing these theoretical perspectives and then develop a model of fear of crime.

RISK AND FEAR IN AN INTERACTIONIST FRAMEWORK

As defined in the last chapter, fear of crime is an emotional response of dread or anxiety to crime or symbols that a person associates with crime. This definition of fear implies that some recognition of potential danger, what we may call perceived risk, is necessary to evoke fear. Thus, a theoretical perspective which stresses the role of risk interpretation would appear to be most helpful in our endeavor. Symbolic interactionism is one theoretical perspective, though not the only one, which may be most illuminating for understanding the role that perceptions of crime risk play in affecting fear. This theoretical perspective will be used to shape the model-building process because the heart of the subject matter is how people gather and interpret information around them regarding victimization potentials and then choose appropriate courses of action. As a theoretical perspective, symbolic interactionism helps one to recognize that social life is viewed as predicated upon the judgments of actors in the course of interaction. People do not act solely on "facts" but work with the information available to them to make sense of their world (Thomas and Thomas 1928).

Interactionism locates the causes of human behavior in what people believe and how they interpret the reality around them. Herbert Blumer, one of the chief architects of contemporary symbolic interactionism, claims that the perspective ultimately rests on three simple premises. Blumer's first premise is that "human beings act toward things on the basis of the meanings that the things have for them" (Blumer 1969, p. 2). This premise is central to symbolic interactionism but is in no way unique to this perspective. However, the second premise differentiates symbolic interactionism from other perspectives by considering the source of the meaning of "things." Blumer contends that George H. Mead— one of the chief architects of interactionism—made it clear that the "meaning of such things is derived from, or arises out of, the social interaction that one has with one's fellows" (Blumer 1969, p. 2, 68–70). Thus, meanings are social products, externalizations of human groups, which help them to define their activities. Third, "meanings are handled in, and modified through, an interpretative process used by the person in dealing with the things he encounters" (Blumer 1969, p. 2). To determine whether one is afraid of crime, therefore, one needs to ascertain what "crime" or specific victimizations mean to the person.[3]

Blumer (1969) goes on to say that "The actor selects, checks, suspends, regroups, and transforms the meanings in light of the situation in which he is placed and the direction of his action" (p. 5). The interpretive process is not conducted in a social vacuum, but rather in a situational context. For W. I. Thomas, the situational context is the key to analyzing any account in social life: "The total situation will always contain more and less subjective factors, and the behavior reaction can be studied only in connection with the whole context, i.e., the situation as it exists in verifiable, objective terms, and as it has seemed to exist in terms of the interested persons" (Thomas and Thomas 1928, p. 572). According to Thomas, any account of social life that does not examine both the "objective" and "subjective" reality is incomplete (see also Blumer 1979). In symbolic interactionism, the *situation* refers to the objective conditions, and the *definition of the situation* refers to the subjective experience of the situation. As it pertains to fear of crime, the situation includes a person's physical location and activities as well as actual crime prevalence, the physical environment, and victimization experiences and reports. A definition of the situation develops for individuals and groups as actors sense and interpret the situation in social context.

Among the first to define the concept, Thomas and Znaniecki (1918) said the definition of the situation is " . . . the more or less clear conception of the conditions and consciousness of the attitudes" held by the individual or group under consideration (p. 68). In short, the definition of the situation is a set of ideas that give meaning to specific attitudes. Later in this same study, *The Polish Peasant in Europe and America*, the authors temper this somewhat reified conceptualization by asserting that the definition of the situation is a two-phase process rather than the externalized product of cognition. In describing this process, they state that the first phase is often quite undetermined and characterized by an essential vagueness. "In the second phase the situation becomes definite, the wish is crystallized and objectified, and the individual begins to control his new experience" (p. 1847).

Thomas's later writings are even more explicit in emphasizing the sequential character of the definition of the situation. As described in *The Unadjusted Girl*: "Preliminary to any self-determined act of behavior there is always a stage of examination and deliberation that we may call the definition of the situation" (Thomas 1923, p. 42). More succinctly, he says that "The definition of the situation is equivalent to the determination of the vague" (p. 81).[4] In sum, there are rival definitions of the situation in most circumstances, and individuals go through a process of evaluating these definitions and act on the basis of these evaluations. Consistent with Blumer (1969) " . . . action on the part of a human being consists of taking account of various things he notes and forging a line of conduct on the basis of how he interprets them" (p. 15). Since the lines of conduct are continually being modified, the definition of the situation is probably best seen as a process (Blumer 1979, pp. 56–57; Charon 1989; Stebbins 1967, 1969).

To illustrate, consider the phenomenon of carjacking—where drivers of cars are either coerced to drive the assailant somewhere, turn over valuables, and/or give up the car. Some carjackers work in groups in a "bump-and-run" operation. For instance, two thieves may follow a potential victim and then intentionally bump the victim's car and wait for the person to exit his or her vehicle, making it easier for one of the thieves to steal the car. Most police and insurance companies know that carjacking is a crime that most often occurs in large cities; they also know that out-of-state travelers are more often victimized. Rental cars are prime targets for carjackers looking for people who appear to be unfamiliar with an area or uncertain of where they are going. Carjackers also know that victims will show less resistance to turning over a rental car than they will to their own vehicle. As a result of fatal carjackings involving tourists, Florida now prohibits rental companies from identifying their rental cars with company names. Although carjacking occurs in America, this does not necessarily mean that all Americans are afraid of being carjacked. The critical question is how people define the situation of driving. In routine travel to work, church, or shopping, people are familiar with routes and carjacking may not even enter their minds. On vacation, in a rental car, however, they may be more careful and vigilant—and perhaps fearful.

Consider fear of AIDS as a parallel example for how people define situations. Actors are only afraid of acquired immune deficiency syndrome once they "take account" of their knowledge of the disease, their likelihood of contracting it, and what it would entail if they contracted it. In judging the situation, the actor examines his or her lifestyle including sexual behavior and possible drug use in order to estimate fear of AIDS. AIDS appears awfully frightening to anyone who contracts it, but only those who *think they are at risk* of contracting the condition will likely be afraid. People who suffer from hemophilia and people who engage in intravenous drug use or promiscuous sexual behavior— be it homosexual or heterosexual—are more likely to be afraid of AIDS, largely because they feel they are at risk of contracting a lethal disease.

Risk, by definition, involves exposure to the chance of loss or injury. Because it entails chance, it represents one example of what Thomas and other symbolic interactionists describe as actors "determining the vague." One can never be sure of the risks of victimization; one can only gather the relevant information and make a judgment about victimization risk (Fischhoff, Bostrom, and Quadrel 1993). Some people may spend more time judging risk of criminal or civil victimization because they interpret their environment to merit such detailed processing, especially when travel occurs at night or when one is alone in places beyond one's "territory" (Melbin 1978; Warr 1990). Higher perceived risk often implies more information seeking and a higher awareness—actors judge the situation as needing higher vigilance.

Actual risk, although never known, is part of the calculus used to interpret the situation, but interactionism posits that what actors *perceive* as important is what will shape subsequent beliefs and behaviors. As Thomas and Thomas (1928) described the importance of the perceptual process, "If men define situations as real, they are real in their consequences" (p. 572).

In symbolic interactionism, the concept of risk is also evident in the development of meaning as definitions of a situation emerge (Thomas 1923; Thomas and Thomas 1928). People bring meanings of objects to interactive settings because of previous experience and may then recalibrate the meaning in light of the current situation or new information (Stebbins 1967; Stryker 1980). Thus, it is often the case that revised meanings serve as "instruments for the guidance and formation of action" (Blumer 1969, p. 5).[5]

Symbolic interactionism emphasizes emergent definitions of risk during the process of interaction rather than definitions of

risk based largely on the actor's psychological and social constitu-
tion. The self no doubt influences this process but does not determine it. For interactionism, a host of personal, structural, and situational variables converge to predispose one toward definitions
of the situation and relevant actions but actors actually make such
judgments and select lines of action during the course of social
activity (Mead 1934).

Fear is only one of several reactions to judgments of potentially high risk in a situation. Others may include constrained
behavior, community or political activism, compensatory defensive actions, and avoidance behaviors including relocation. Perceived risk and the possible reactions to it are viewed as always
being developed in an environmental context replete with socially
constructed meanings. As Blumer (1969) notes: "human beings
act toward things on the basis of the meanings that the things have
for them" (p. 2). Thus, actors may develop meanings for certain
environments that emphasize security, concern, rest, or active
monitoring. The actor develops such meanings using two broad
classes of stimuli: physical and cultural.

First, physical environments, and the spatial relationships
encompassed in them, are crucial to actors in the process of defining or labeling zones of activity (Hall 1966; Lewis and Salem
1986; Wilson 1983; Wilson and Kelling 1982). Actors judge environments on a number of relevant domains and definitions of
those zones emerge (LaGory and Pipkin 1981). Familiarity with
the environment is crucial because people are more likely to judge
unfamiliar environments as requiring more vigilance and, in some
cases, as generating more fear (Taylor, Gottfredson, and Brower
1984). Second, cultural artifacts, structures, and processes give
meaning to judgments about environments. Both expert and scientific knowledge as well as folk knowledge contribute our stock
of available information.

While a symbolic interactionist approach articulates well how
actors judge situations and how definitions of the situation
emerge, there are other theoretical perspectives which have much
to offer in elaborating how a nebulous "environment" influences
this process. In other words, there is value in considering other
theoretical perspectives to better understand how a host of environmental forces shapes definitions of the situation. In doing so, I
seek to, at least in part, span the gulf from micro- to macro-socio-
logical levels of analysis in considering reactions to crime. Two

perspectives, which vary considerably in their degree of theoretical development, have been selected for consideration here: incivility and criminal opportunity.

CONVERGING THEORETICAL PERSPECTIVES IN AN ENVIRONMENTAL CONTEXT

What has been articulated thus far about judgments of the environmental context bears many similarities to what has come to be known as the *incivility* hypothesis (Lewis and Maxfield 1980; Lewis and Salem 1986; Wilson 1983; Wilson and Kelling 1982). Scholars from a variety of fields including criminology, geography, policy studies, psychology, and sociology have long recognized that various features of the physical environment are related to criminal realities. Some places develop reputations for being crime prone not only because of past criminal episodes but also because of "signs of crime" (Skogan 1990; Skogan and Maxfield 1981). These signs of crime are most often features of the physical environment which serve as cues to actors that risk may be higher. Therefore, most people structure their lives to avoid the most risky environments, especially at certain times of day. For example, when urban places have repeated manifestations of graffiti, broken windows, abandoned or burned-out buildings, and homeless persons, they often become characterized as places of "urban unease" (Wilson 1968) or "incivility" (Hunter 1978). In popular vernacular, these places are called "slums."

Studies of urban transitions, suburbanization, and social disorganization have long considered how features of the physical environment affect community perceptions of social organization and social change (Park and Burgess 1925 [1967]). Wilson and Kelling's (1985) discussion of broken windows developed this notion between violations of appearance and public reactions to them. Not only is incivility related to social disorder and criminal victimization but they posit that incivility influences fear of crime: "we tend to overlook or forget another source of fear—the fear of being bothered by disorderly people. Not violent people, nor, necessarily, criminals, but disreputable or obstreperous or unpredictable people" (p. 221).

It is becoming fairly well established in the literature that incivility actually has two domains spanning the physical environ-

Figure 2.1. Evaluating Incivility
Judging the level of incivility in an area is something we do quickly and
often. Here are two residential areas from the same city which probably
spark disparate estimates of neighborhood civility.

ment and the social environment. Following LaGrange, Ferraro, and Supancic (1992), incivility is defined here as "low-level breaches of community standards that signal an erosion of conventionally accepted norms and values" (p. 312). *Physical incivility* refers to disorderly physical surroundings such as litter, abandoned buildings or cars, graffiti, broken or barricaded windows, and unkept lots. *Social incivility* refers to disruptive social behaviors such as the presence of rowdy youth, homeless people, beggars, drunks ("riffraff" on the streets) or, perhaps, inconsiderate neighbors. Based on previous studies, both physical and social incivility should heighten fear of crime, although their effects are probably indirect via heightened perceived risk of crime (LaGrange, Ferraro, and Supancic 1992). Some studies have used both researcher-defined standards of incivility while other studies used subject-defined standards. The latter have shown stronger effects on perceptions of crime (Covington and Taylor 1991) suggesting that even definitions of incivility are socially constructed. People rarely witness criminal episodes but we routinely observe the signs of incivility. In this sense, the incivility literature is beneficial to the interactionist framework developed here as people use information about the environment, including its degree of incivility, in estimating risk; the higher the perceived incivility, the greater the estimate of risk due to criminal victimization.[6]

A second theoretical perspective which can be judiciously integrated with symbolic interaction theory is known as *criminal opportunity* theory (Cohen and Felson 1979). This perspective extends the consideration of ecological influence even further. I began with a theoretical perspective, symbolic interactionism, which is primarily classified as a micro-sociological framework. While the incivility hypothesis helps to include environmental influence, criminal opportunity theory permits even greater inclusion of how macrostructural and geographical forces affect how individuals define situations as potentially dangerous.

Criminal opportunity theory, often referred to as routine activities theory, has most often been applied at the macrostructural level in research on crime (e.g., Stahura and Sloan 1988). Yet, there is no compelling reason why the theory cannot be applied in tandem with a primarily microsociological perspective such as symbolic interactionism (see Cohen and Felson [1979] for discussion and application at both levels of analysis). Indeed, one contribution of the present research is to consider both macro and micro levels of analysis in explaining the distribution and etiology of fear of crime. Macrostructural features of the environment and social life shape interpretive and behavioral processes. Yet macro structures and process are incapable of totally explaining why people perceive of criminal realities the way they do.

Although originally developed to explain why people engage in crime, routine activities or criminal opportunity theory may be adapted to help understand risk and fear of crime. It suggests that potential offenders make "rational" choices about various criminal opportunities in the environment (Hindelang, Gottfredson, and Garofalo 1978; Cohen and Felson 1979; Cohen, Felson, and Land 1980; Stahura and Hollinger 1988). Potential offenders are likely to be drawn to targets which offer high reward but comparatively little risk. According to Cohen and Felson (1979), changing social structures affect the likelihood that potential criminals will prey on targets given the routine activities within regions, neighborhoods, and housing quarters. They argue that crime, especially direct predatory violations, will be highest when three factors converge in time and space: (1) motivated offenders, (2) suitable targets, and (3) an absence of capable guardians to prevent a violation (p. 589).

Cohen and Felson (1979) drew heavily from ecological theory (Hawley 1950) in developing the perspective, noting that criminal opportunities are highly related to lifestyles and social organization. In short, potential offenders judge the risk of crime in an ecological framework and act accordingly, attempting to take advantage of criminal opportunities (Beasley and Antunes 1974; Bursik and Grasmick 1993; Bursik and Webb 1982; Harris 1976).

Just as the criminal opportunity perspective has been used to model how potential offenders judge the risk of violations, it may also be useful to conceptualize how *potential victims* may make use of such information in judging their risk of victimization. In other words, while potential offenders may take advantage of information about living quarters, crime rates, police protection, and neighborhood surveillance in judging the risk of a violation, potential victims may likewise use such information to judge the threat of being victimized.

People estimate risk of crime by observing numerous ecological indicators such as "broken windows," surveillance efforts, and poverty. Of course, social class is one of the most basic pieces of information people use to judge risk in a neighborhood or community. Neighborhoods characterized by a high degree of incivility are almost always neighborhoods with a large proportion of lower-class residents. Yet, other factors besides social class help to define the level of incivility. Knowledge of previous crimes also informs people's current judgments of crime risk. Places develop reputations, among both potential victims and offenders, based on criminal activity and efforts to constrain crime. While people may not have completely accurate knowledge of crime prevalence, they nonetheless have an image of areas as good or bad (LaGory and Pipken 1981; Pyle 1990). Also, some cities develop reputations as high crime places (e.g., Washington, DC, Detroit).

To summarize the theoretical approach applied here, there is an ecological structure to criminal opportunities, and these opportunities are estimated by both potential offenders and victims. At the same time that ecological forces operate to shape risk of victimization, there is also the interpretive process whereby individuals consider these factors in light of the biography and resources of the self (Stryker 1980). To capture both the ecological forces which enhance criminal opportunities and the interpretive process potential victims use to estimate risk and react to it, symbolic interactionism is integrated with the incivility and criminal opportunity frameworks into a *risk interpretation* model.

This theoretical model is an attempt to bridge the gap between micro- and macro-levels of analysis (Alexander, Giesen, Munch, and Smelser 1987). As Coleman (1990) notes in the *Foundations of Social Theory*, understanding social history and current social life necessitates accounting for the transitions between the micro- and macro-levels of structure and change. I envision macro-structural and ecological conditions and public information sources affecting perceptions of risk and small-group interactions; these small-group interactions are used by the participants to garner additional information regarding victimization potentials and to discuss behavioral change. These micro-level processes, in turn, shape community definitions of safety, disorder, and decline and the media reports which treat such perceptions and victimization events. In sum, crime prevalence and community traits affect perceived risk, behavioral adaptations, and fear but these personal and interpersonal phenomena eventually act back on community traits and crime prevalence as evidenced in media reports and community organization.

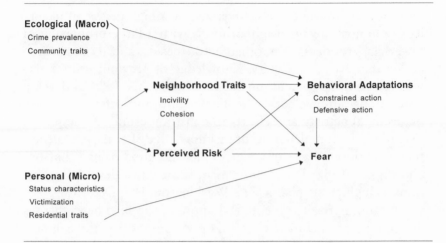

Figure 2–2
Generic Model of Fear of Crime Based on
a Risk Interpretation Approach

As Coleman (1990) and others have demonstrated, there are clearly cycles of transitions from macro to micro and back to macro structures and processes. Identifying those transitions requires longitudinal data and is beyond the scope of this project. While I hope to collect such data in the future, my current focus is on how macro- and micro-level factors shape individual perceptions and behavioral change as people assess victimization potentials. To that end, Figure 2–2 is presented to summarize the risk interpretation theoretical model.

Macro-level ecological forces play a salient role in the causal framework but the individual's judgments about criminal risk are not omitted. Ecological factors include information about previous crimes, criminal opportunities, and community organization garnered from the media, neighbors, peers, and observation of human activity patterns. Personal factors influencing people's judgments of risk of crime include personal victimization, personal knowledge of other's victimization, and the resources available to deal with a potential threat (resources include health, living quarters, and neighborhood assistance, to name a few). Both the ecological and personal characteristics are seen as shaping perceptions of neighborhood incivility and cohesion. Neighborhood incivility and cohesion are probably negatively related but this is always dependent upon *perceptions* of neighborhood characteristics. These perceptions of neighborhood characteristics, in turn, affect perceived risk. In considering both ecological and personal characteristics, the meanings that actors learn and attribute to these phenomena are crucial in assessing risk of criminal victimization. Perceptions of neighborhood characteristics and risk of victimization may produce a variety of outcomes. The one emphasized here is fear but behavioral adaptations may also occur. People may constrain their actions or adopt defensive actions to deal with perceived high risk, but the nature of the relationship between behavioral adaptations and fear is difficult to predict. Previous studies give contradictory findings. One study suggests that there is a reciprocal relationship between fear and constrained behavior such that an escalating loop exists (Liska, Sanchirico, & Reed 1988) while another test of nonrecursive or "feedback" models shows that fear increases defensive actions but that such defensive actions do not further heighten fear (Taylor et al. 1986). Further attention will be given to testing these and other alternatives in chapter five.[7]

This risk interpretation model could also be adapted to explain other behaviors involving risk such as residential and social mobility or the risk of health-related activities. For example, when it comes to health, people are continually making decisions about the relative risks from ecological and personal forces. Ecological concerns might include air and water quality, congestion, electromagnetic or radioactive fields, sick-building syndrome, and crime. Personal factors would include genetic and lifestyle influences, where lifestyle would include a host of health-destructive and health-protective behaviors ranging from dietary to occupational activities (Langlie 1977; Becker and Rosenstock 1989). Similarly, judgments about health risks may precipitate behavioral change, fatalism, or fear. Before pondering the suitability of the model for explaining other phenomena, however, our next step, and the aim of chapter 3, is to systematically examine this model in light of previous research on fear of crime. A review of the current state of knowledge is in order if the model has any hope of extending our understanding.

CHAPTER 3

Measuring Risk and Fear of Crime

Unfettered thought is the essence of research methods.
Stanislav Andreski

It has been said that "measurement is the basis of all science." It should not be surprising, then, that a scientific discussion of fear of crime must invariably consider how it and related concepts have been defined and measured in previous research. This chapter begins by reviewing the extant literature on fear of crime in light of the risk interpretation model while giving special attention to issues of measurement. It concludes by introducing the survey data and measures of risk and fear which will be used to extend our understanding of how people interpret victimization chances.

There are two overarching criticisms of much of the previous literature which will be examined in detail. The first is the lack of specificity in defining and measuring fear of crime. The second is the related problem of omitting perceived risk from models of how people interpret potential victimization. While the order of presenting them here may be somewhat arbitrary, the question of how fear of crime is defined and measured seems so rudimentary that it may be an apropos starting place. In addition, once the problems with defining and measuring fear of crime are articulated, the reasons for the omission of perceived risk from many previous studies will become fairly obvious.

DEFINING AND MEASURING FEAR OF CRIME

While defining fear of crime appears to be an elementary step in doing research on the subject, the dearth of explicit definitions for it was one of the main reasons I originally started this stream of research. I was shocked that so many investigators apparently assumed that a definition of fear of crime was obvious, and I found others who shared my sense of frustration. For instance,

21

DuBow, McCabe, and Kaplan (1979) identified the problem: "'fear of crime' refers to a wide variety of subjective and emotional assessments and behavioral reports. There is a serious lack of both consistency and specificity in these reports" (p. 1). Garofalo and Laub (1978) asserted that "what has been measured in research as the 'fear of crime' is simply not fear of crime" (p. 246). It would be an understatement to say that the term "fear of crime" has been casually used in the research literature. Warr (1984) summarized the problem well when he stated that: "the phrase 'fear of crime' has acquired so many divergent meanings in the literature that it is in danger of losing any specificity whatsoever" (p. 681). He then stated his preference for the phrase "fear of victimization." In short, there is considerable confusion among many researchers—let alone the public and policymakers—over what "fear of crime" really is. If there are no clear and widely accepted definitions of the concept, then it becomes easy for various studies to reify the existence of "fear" among certain groups (e.g., older people).

Despite the lack of and confusion over definitions of fear of crime, one finds surprising consistency in the way it has been measured in dozens of studies. Although variation exists, the core of the literature centers around the indicators used in two surveys. This is probably due to the widespread access to the surveys which contain these indicators. The two surveys with the accompanying questions are: (1) National Crime Survey (NCS), "How safe do you feel or would you feel being out alone in your neighborhood at night?" [parallel question for "during the day?"] and (2) General Social Survey (GSS), "Is there any area right around here— that is, within a mile—where you would be afraid to walk alone at night?"[1] The second question is the most frequently used measure of fear of crime in the literature (Ferraro and LaGrange 1987). Critiques of the use of these measures as indicators of fear of crime are presented elsewhere (Ferraro and LaGrange 1987, 1992), but one of the most fundamental problems with them, especially the NCS measure, is the failure to distinguish fear from perceived risk of crime (see also Schwarzenegger 1991, 1992).

In an attempt to clarify the definition of fear of crime, Table 3–1 is presented as a conceptual framework for defining various perceptions about crime (reprinted from Ferraro and LaGrange 1988). The classification is adapted from DuBow et al. (1979) and includes an example of the type of question for each of the six cells (see also Ferraro and LaGrange 1987). The vertical axis refers to the level of reference of crime perceptions. These range from the general (i.e., community-oriented) to the personal (i.e., self-oriented). The horizontal axis refers to the type of crime perception and ranges from the cognitive (what we think) to the affective (what we feel). The cognitive dimension on the left end of the continuum encompasses assessments of risk and safety while the affective dimension on the right includes feelings of fear. Finally, different combinations of the level of reference and the type of crime perception in Table 3-1 are represented by cells A through F.

As stated in the previous chapter, I define fear of crime as an emotional response of dread or anxiety to crime or symbols that a person associates with crime (Ferraro and LaGrange 1987, p. 71; Garofalo 1981, p. 840; LaGrange and Ferraro 1987). Note from Table 3-1 that only cells C and F represent the emotional state of fear (including worry) of the respondent; cell C represents fear for others who may be victimized and cell F represents fear for oneself—what many "fear of crime" researchers assume they are measuring. Cells B and E represent concern about crime (e.g., whether the respondent thinks crime is a serious social problem), and cells A and D represent perceived risk of being victimized by crime.

When reviewing previous research on fear of crime, it is apparent that many studies do not differentiate between perceived risk and fear. Some studies combine perceived risk and fear measures into constructs which are then labelled fear (e.g., Brantingham, Brantingham, and Butcher 1986; Taylor, Taub, and Peterson 1986). Although the two concepts are no doubt related, they are, nonetheless, distinct phenomena. A person may judge his or her risk of crime to be high but not necessarily be afraid. While the NCS measures are often used as indicators of fear, it is possible that they may be even better indicators of perceived risk (Ferraro and LaGrange 1992). At the very least, the NCS measures probably assesses a blend of the two concepts of perceived risk and fear. Yin (1980) comments on the lack of definitions of fear of crime and the likelihood that the measures so often used have low validity: "Though fear of crime is almost never explicitly defined by researchers, their measurements suggest that such fear is implicitly defined as the perception of the probability of being victimized" (p. 496, emphasis added). In other words, there is a rampant confounding of fear and perceived risk in research on the subject,

Table 3-1

Classification and Examples of Crime Perceptions

	Type of Perception		
	Cognitive		Affective
Level of Reference	Judgments	Values	Emotions
General	A.	B.	C.
	Risk to others; crime or safety assessments	Concern about crime to others	Fear for others' victimization
	Do you think that people in this neighborhood are safe inside their homes at night? (Clarke and Lewis 1982)	Choose the single most serious domestic problem (from a list of 10) that you would like to see government do something about. (Furstenberg 1971)	I worry a great deal about the safety of my loved ones from crime and criminals. (Lee 1982a)
Personal	D.	E.	F.
	Risk to self; safety of self	Concern about crime to self; personal intolerance	Fear for self-victimization
	How safe do you feel or would you feel being alone in your neighborhood at night? (Liksa et al. 1982)	Are you personally concerned about becoming a victim of crime? (Jaehnig et al.1981)	How afraid are you of becoming the victim of (16 separate offenses) in your everyday life? (Warr and Stafford 1983)

Reprinted from Ferraro and LaGrange [1988], adapted from DuBow et al. [1979].

especially among researchers using the National Crime Survey item(s).

Fear is a fundamentally different psychological experience than perceived risk. While risk entails a cognitive judgment, fear is far more emotive in character. Fear activates a series of complex bodily changes alerting the actor to the possibility of danger. The bodily changes, particularly in the endocrine system, can be either functional or dysfunctional to the actor (Sarnoff and Zimbardo 1961; Silberman 1981). Fear may release adrenalin and empower actors to accomplish special feats of defense or flight. On the other hand, the bodily changes can be counterproductive resulting in physiological dysfunction, especially if experienced repeatedly as a *chronic* stressor (Selye 1956, 1974; Stagner 1981). Goffman (1971, p. 4) differentiates fear from "dissociated vigilance" which involves monitoring the environment during daily activities:

> They go about their business grazing, gazing, mothering, digesting, building, resting, playing, placidly attending to easily managed matters at hand. Or, full mobilized, a fury of intent, alarmed, they get ready to attack or to stalk or to flee.

Given that fear involves an emotional, and sometimes physiological, reaction to perceived danger, there exists an inherent difficulty in measuring fear from questionnaire or interview data collection methods. Whereas experimental data on fear experiences are either not ethical to collect or likely to have limited validity from "laboratory simulations," even the best survey measures of fear of crime are not pure reflections of emotional experiences. Rather, they are expressions of imagined fear.[2] Stated differently, survey questions ask people to "imaginatively rehearse" a line of action (Mead 1934). While there are no ideal survey measures of fear of crime that would be available for a population on all types of victimization, one should expect that the measures emphasize the emotional reaction to a given victimization rather than an estimate of perceived risk. Clearly, the measures for fear and perceived risk should *not* be interchangeable.

Beyond the limitations of previous research using questionable measures of fear of crime, there is also a propensity to use single-item indicators as the outcome measures. Some studies, such as those using the General Social Survey item, only have one variable, while others have more than one variable but analyze them individually—for whatever reasons. While this is not always a problem, one difficulty of single item measures is that reliability is unknown. Thus, not only are some of the measures questionable on the grounds of validity, but reliability is often tenuous. We do know, however, that when analyzing data, "unreliability in a partialled variable may yield grossly inaccurate results when it is ignored" (Cohen and Cohen 1975, p. 372).

Only Crime at Night?

Coupled with the problems of validity and reliability of some of the most commonly used measures of fear of crime are the problems of references to "crime" and "night" in most questions. First, crime is not defined in many questions but left for respondents to designate. As such, "crime" may be more likely to conjure up images of personal or violent crime (LaGrange and Ferraro 1987). The NCS item asking about safety does not even use the word crime in the question. In all fairness, it is imbedded in a "crime survey" and probably *implies* crime but the lack of specificity is alarming given its widespread use.

Some studies using alternative measures ask about different victimizations and show wide variation in the degree of fear associated with the types of crime. For instance, Warr (1984) finds that fear of victimization varies according to the offense considered and by gender. For men, mean levels of fear on a scale of 0 to 10 (with 0 indicating the least amount of fear) ranged across 16 offenses from .5 for "being beat up by someone you know" to 5.48 for "having someone break into your home while you're away." For women, mean levels of fear ranged from 1.52 for "being beat up by someone you know" to 6.18 for "having someone break into your home while you're away." While it is somewhat assuring that the victimizations are the same for both men and women on the lowest and highest mean values of fear, the variation across victimizations is substantial indeed. Given such variation, it is hard to determine what generic references to "crime" actually mean in single-item questions such as the GSS indicator.

Second, the tilt toward violent or personal crime in both the NCS and GSS items is further shaped by the reference to nighttime activity. Actually, the NCS asks a parallel question for daytime activity but many investigators do not use it. Warr (1990) has masterfully shown that night triggers different reactions to the prospect of being on the streets. Therefore, what does this mean about the extant research using the night items? It probably solidifies the subject's reference to violent personal "street" crime and forces a substantial number of the respondents to imaginatively rehearse a situation they never experience. Do women specifically avoid being out alone at night within one mile of their home? If yes, then the GSS asks them to think about their fear for a situation they purposely avoid. Does that truly represent their fear of crime? In reality they may not fear the situation because they know they are not very likely to be in it. Rather, they avoid it because they judge its *risk* to be high, and the item forces many people to imaginatively rehearse situations they rarely experience.

While it may now be clear what is wrong with previous measures purporting to measure fear of crime, it may be judicious to briefly emphasize how to develop sound measures for future research (see also Ferraro and LaGrange 1987). First, measures of fear of crime should tap the emotional state of fear or worry rather than judgments or concerns about crime. Second, explicit reference to the type of crime or victimization is necessary—questions should avoid generic references to "crime." Third, questions should be aimed at assessing the phenomena in the subject's everyday life—not hypothetical or purposefully avoided situations. It may be useful to include a statement about the subject's "everyday life" so as to let the respondents define their daily activities and routines. Fourth, in a related vein, avoid double-barrelled items such as the NCS's "How safe *do you or would you* feel" (emphasis added), which obscure the target object. Fifth, multiple items that span a range of seriousness for victimizations will enable researchers to compare types of crime as well as to create overall factors or indexes of fear of crime. Finally, if as suggested here, risk is seen as a pivotal concept in the development of fear of crime, then researchers might want to consider creating parallel items for perceived risk and fear (Ferraro and LaGrange 1992; Warr and Stafford 1983). Indeed, it may be useful to now turn our attention to defining and measuring risk of crime.

RISK OF CRIME: DEFINITION AND MEASUREMENT

Despite the logic of considering perceived risk as a predictor of fear of crime and the implicit discussion of risk in previous literature, numerous studies do not directly measure perceived risk of crime (e.g., Liska, Sanchirico, and Reed 1988).[3] Based upon our earlier discussion of measurement, researchers for many of these studies used indicators which probably measured perceived risk but interpreted those measures as reflecting fear. Others have mixed indicators of perceived risk with fear and then label the construct fear (e.g., Taylor, Taub, and Peterson 1986), certainly a practice which is less than state of the art (Bankston et al. 1990; Fattah and Sacco 1989; Ferraro and LaGrange 1992; Lee 1982b; Warr 1984, 1990).

Among the studies which have incorporated the concept of risk, there are two basic approaches. First, some researchers have used official crime statistics to provide an estimate of "objective" or "official" crime risk (e.g., Janson and Ryder 1983). Crime rates for police precincts, Census tracts, aggregates of precincts or tracts, and counties have all been used in previous research. Although official statistics are subject to bias—generally underestimating the prevalence of crime—they do provide one way of attempting to link known risks with fear. Second, some scholars have asked respondents to estimate their own risk of victimization—what may be termed "subjective" or "perceived" risk. This has been done in reference to "personal" and "property" crime (e.g., LaGrange and Ferraro 1989) or for batteries of specific victimizations to parallel the fear measures (e.g., Ferraro and LaGrange 1992; Warr and Stafford 1983).

Perceived risk, according to DuBow et al. (1979, p. 3) refers to people's assessments of crime rates and the probability of victimization. While people's estimates of victimization risk may not correlate well with official statistics, some argue that perceived risk is a better measure if one is attempting to predict fear. The perceived risk measure may account for one's routine activities, resources, and location in a larger area used to collect crime statistics. Each approach has its advantages and limitations but both attempt to link how the occurrence of crime affects a person's fear of victimization.

Table 3–2 is presented to summarize the studies which have incorporated risk of crime—either official or perceived—in attempting to understand "fear" of crime. (Excluded from this listing are studies which do not explicitly discuss "fear" of crime and those which report official crime risk but do not incorporate it into the analysis [e.g., Maxfield 1984].) I regard the list of twenty-nine studies to be fairly comprehensive but not exhaustive of previous research. In many ways, I regard the studies listed in Table 3–2 as exemplars for advancing our scientific understanding of how people interpret criminal realities and victimization potentials because, unlike dozens of others, they attempt to incorporate risk while studying fear. On the other hand, many of the studies have serious shortcomings which suggest the need for and

Table 3–2

Previous Research on "Fear" of Crime Incorporating Risk of Crime: Study, Age Range, Sample Location, and Measures Used

	Measurement		
Study; ages; location	Official Risk	Perceived Risk	Fear
Baker et al., 1983; NA[a]; Phoenix	Change past year	None	GSS[b]; modified GSS
Bankston & Thompson, 1989; 15+; Louisiana	None	5-item index	5-item index
Box et al. 1988; 16+; United Kingdom	None	Victimization likelihood	Modified GSS[b]
Brantingham et al., 1986; 20+; Vancouver, BC	9 offenses	None; mixed with fear	4-item index; risk & fear mixed
Ferraro & LaGrange, 1992; 18+; U.S.	None	10-item index; 2 latent variables	10-item index; 2 latent variables
Furstenberg, 1971; NA[a]; Baltimore, MD	Overall rate	None; see fear	8-item index; perceived risk for fear
Giles-Sims, 1984; 60+; Texas county	None	5-item index; personal/prop.	4-item index; 2 latent variables
Hartnagel, 1979; 18+; Edmonton, Alb	None	Change in violent crime	2 items; city, neighborhood
Hindelang et al., 1978; 12+; 8 U.S. cities	None	Change; 2 items	NCS[c]
Janson & Ryder, 1983; 45–74; Los Angeles	7 offenses	None	3-item index, crime concern
Jaycox, 1978; 60+; 4 U.S. cities	None	3 items[d]	3 items[d]
LaGrange & Ferraro, 1989; 18+; North Carolina County	None	2 items; personal, property	11-item index; 2 latent variables
LaGrange et al., 1992; 18+; U.S.	None	10-item index; 2 latent variables	10-item index; 2 latent variables
Lawton & Yaffe, 1980; elderly; U.S.[e]	8 offenses	None	26-item index, fear

Table 3–2 (continued)

Study; ages; location	Measurement		
	Official Risk	Perceived Risk	Fear
Lee, 1982a; 55+; State of Washington	None	4-item index	7-item factor variable
Lewis & Maxfield, 1980; NA[a]; Chicago	4 offenses	4 items	Modified NCS[c]
McPherson, 1978; NA[a]; Minneapolis	6 offenses	6 items	Nighttime danger in neighborhood
Miethe & Lee, 1984; 55+; State of Washington	2 offenses	2 violent items 2 property items	2 violent items, 2 property items
Ortega & Myles, 1987; NA[a]; Chicago	Neighborhood (high/low)	Neighborhood risk	GSS[b]
Riger et al., 1978; NA[a]; NCS, 3 U.S. cities	Rape	Rape risk	NCS[c]
Schwarzenegger, 1991; 16+; Zurich, Switz.	None	Victim prognosis	GSS, daytime "GSS"
Stafford & Galle, 1984; NA[a]; Chicago	4 offenses, victimization	None	NCS[c] item
Sundeen & Mathieu, 1976; 52+; 3 California areas	None	Safety 1-item	4 items, anxiety
Taylor, D., et al., 1986; NA[a]; Chicago	personal; property	None; mixed with fear	4-item latent factor mixes risk and worry
Taylor, R., & Hale, 1986; NA[a]; Atlanta	8 offenses	None	3-item factor, general; 5-item factor, robbery
Taylor, R., et al., 1984; NA[a]; Baltimore	police calls; 7 offenses	None	2-item NCS index[c]
Thomas & Hyman, 1977; NA[a]; East Virginia	None	4-item index	9-item index; mixes fear and risk
Warr, 1984; 19+; Seattle	None	16 items	16 items
Warr & Stafford, 1983; 19+; Seattle	None	16 items	16 items

Note: Additional studies which simply compare crime rates with public estimates direction of future research. For each study, the age range and location of the sample are listed along with the way in which risk and fear were measured.

To begin, only five of the twenty-nine studies use both official and perceived risk data in predicting fear of crime; most use one approach or the other. Consider first the fourteen studies which use official risk statistics or crime rates in their analyses. Several studies which include official statistics on crimes known to the police (not arrest data) show a significant effect on "fear" of crime (e.g., Janson and Ryder 1983; Lawton and Yaffe 1980). In these studies which report a significant effect, the magnitude of the effect due to official risk is rarely the largest.[4] Other studies using official statistics do not report significant direct effects of risk on fear, once controlling for other factors (Miethe and Lee 1984; Taylor and Hale 1986).

When one turns to the twenty studies using perceived risk, most of those studies find perceived risk to be quite predictive of fear of crime, even after controlling for related variables (e.g., Giles-Sims 1984; LaGrange and Ferraro 1989; Miethe and Lee 1984; Warr and Stafford 1983). For instance, when Giles-Sims (1984) added perceived risk to models, she found that no other independent variables affected fear of crime among a sample of older adults living in Tarrant County, Texas. In the only national survey to consider perceived risk, it was found to be a fairly strong predictor of fear of crime (r = .56, beta = .50 [Ferraro and LaGrange 1992; LaGrange et al. 1992]).

When one considers the five studies which include both official and perceived crime risk, the limits of our stock of knowledge become more clear. Four of those five studies were conducted in one of four cities (Chicago, Minneapolis, Philadelphia, and San

---

of crime (e.g., Warr 1980) and those which do not offer multivariate analyses involving risk and fear are excluded (e.g., Cook and Cook 1976; Jaehnig et al. 1981). The studies listed purport to measure fear of crime as evidenced by the title of the manuscript and/or textual references. Studies which include both official crime (crime rates) and perceived risk are *italicized.*

[a]Not available; adults assumed.

[b]General Social Survey; NORC.

[c]National Crime Survey.

[d]It was not clear if and how some authors differentiated perceived risk and fear. Measurement was, therefore, defined according to the schema presented earlier.

[e]Fifty-three public housing sites in thirty-eight U.S. communities.

Francisco).[5] Only the study by Miethe and Lee (1984) includes rural residents, based upon a survey of adults in the state of Washington. As mentioned earlier, the present study's use of national data will add something quite unique to our stock of knowledge.

Next, consider how fear of crime is measured in these five studies. Four out of the five use a form of the National Crime Survey item or the General Social Survey item—a practice now widely acknowledged as less than stellar. Again, only the article by Miethe and Lee (1984) is distinctive, this time because it uses fear items with reasonable levels of validity and reliability. They created two-item indexes for fear of violent crime and fear of property crime, each with alpha reliability coefficients over .74. They also created two-item indexes for perceived risk of violent crime and perceived risk of property crime, each with alpha reliability coefficients over .77. Official risk was measured by county-level rates for aggravated assault and burglary to reflect violent and property risk respectively. Their results showed that the effect of official crime risk was not strong and largely indirect via perceived risk. In addition, they found that fear of property crime was more predictable, especially from the crime-related variables.

Although the other four studies are seriously limited by the measures of fear used, some findings are intriguing and informative. First, Lewis and Maxfield (1980) studied four Chicago neighborhoods and concluded that perceptions of incivility—indicating weakness of social control—were most influential in affecting crime perceptions. Both Lewis and Maxfield (1980) and McPherson (1978) report considerable public accuracy in judging overall crime risk but knowledge of the types of crime prevalence were less accurate. Riger et al. (1978) explored why women generally have higher fear of crime despite lower victimization rates and show that fear of rape overshadows virtually all victimizations for women.

As mentioned earlier, each of the studies offers something to our understanding of fear of crime. I regard Miethe and Lee's (1984) study as an exemplar in many ways. Yet, even it does not examine the possible role of incivility as suggested by a risk interpretation model and it is limited by both geographic region and the types of crime considered. The proposed study incorporates measures of neighborhood incivility as strongly recommended by Lewis and Maxfield (1980). The present study will extend the literature by (a) providing state-of-the-art measurement of perceived risk and fear of crime on a nationally representative sample and *(b)* including both official crime statistics and measures of neighborhood incivility and cohesion in the analysis. It will provide the scientific community with hitherto unavailable information for understanding how people interpret crime and potential victimization.

THE FEAR OF CRIME IN AMERICA SURVEY: METHOD AND MEASURES

Sample

As part of a long-term research program, data were collected on perceived risk and fear of crime during 1990 with the support of the AARP Andrus Foundation. The original project focussed on age differences in fear of crime, not just among older people, but by comparing older and younger persons' levels of fear (Ferraro and LaGrange 1992). Details of sampling and data collection are presented in Appendix A; only a synopsis is given here.

The Fear of Crime in America Survey was conducted via telephone interviews by the Public Opinion Laboratory at Northern Illinois University based on a multistage cluster sampling design with 150 primary sampling units (PSUs). It was structured so that each adult in the United States living in a household with a telephone had an equal chance of being selected for the sample. Within each household, one respondent was randomly selected and interviewed with a computer-assisted telephone interviewing system (EQ^{tm}, Electronic Questionnaire). The primary bias in the sampling frame is that some individuals do not have telephones; most census data estimates indicate, however, that this group is only about 4 percent and is a highly transient population that is difficult to sample by any method.

A final sample of 1,101 respondents was obtained with a response rate of 61 percent. This sample approximates the national noninstitutionalized population across several key variables but has a somewhat higher proportion of metropolitan residents (84% in this sample compared to 77% for the population; U.S. Bureau of the Census 1989). The gender distribution is 55 percent women and 45 percent men. Eighty-four percent of the sample are white, about nine percent are African Americans, and approximately four percent are Hispanic Americans. The mean age is 44.3 with about 15 percent of the sample at least 65 years of age. Ninety-one percent are high-school graduates but only about 31 percent are college graduates. About 19 percent of the respondents reported being victimized during the previous year. Interviews consisted of approximately seventy questions and averaged about fifteen minutes (ranging from ten to thrity minutes).

Measures

As we were designing the survey, we were certain that the questions to be used to measure fear of crime had to meet the criteria we established in earlier research (e.g., Ferraro and LaGrange 1987) and to resemble closely those items which we identified as exemplars of sound measurement of the concept (Warr and Stafford 1983). The questions used to measure fear of crime are presented in Table 3–3. The ten victimizations were selected to span the range of personal and property crimes. A "scale from 1 to 10" was selected to assure sufficient variation in a widely understood strategy.[6] As noted earlier, we recommended that parallel questions be used for perceived risk as well. The introduction to and samples of the perceived risk of crime measures are also presented in Table 3–3. These questions are similar to those used by Warr (1984) in a self-administered format. (See Appendix B for the entire interview schedule with descriptive statistics.)

The focal endogenous variables—fear of crime questions— were asked early in the interview schedule. The fear and risk items were not contiguous in the interview so that respondents would not try to recall their rating for fear of a crime when assessing risk for the same crime. Five questions separated each battery of victimizations. As will be shown in later chapters, other questions were asked to measure concepts which were suggested by previous research and which fit within the risk interpretation model (e.g., neighborhood incivility).

MODELING FEAR AND PERCEIVED RISK

First, the simple correlations between the separate indicators of fear of crime and risk of crime were examined (these matrices as well as other supplementary tables are presented in Appendix C;

Table 3–3
Measures of Fear and Perceived Risk of Crime

A. FEAR OF CRIME

At one time or another, most of us have experienced fear about becoming the victim of crime. Some crimes probably frighten you more than others. We are interested in *how afraid* people are in everyday life of being a victim of different kinds of crimes. Please rate your fear on a scale of 1 to 10 where 1 means you are *not afraid at all* and 10 means you are *very afraid*.

First, rate your fear of . . .

1. Being approached on the street by a beggar or panhandler.
2. Being cheated, conned, or swindled out of your money.
3. Having someone break into your home while you are away.
4. Having someone break into your home while you are there.
5. Being raped or sexually assaulted.
6. Being murdered.
7. Being attacked by someone with a weapon.
8. Having your car stolen.
9. Being robbed or mugged on the street.
10. Having your property damaged by vandals.

Items were asked in the above order. Three percent of the respondents reported not having a car; their responses were recoded to the mean. All ten items summed for the general fear index (Cronbach's alpha = .90). Items 4, 5, 6, and 7 summed for fear of personal crime index (alpha = .90). Items 2, 3, 8, 9, and 10 summed for the fear of property crime index (alpha = .82).

B. PERCEIVED RISK OF CRIME

You have already rated your fear of different kinds of crimes; now I want you to rate *the chance that a specific thing will happen to you during the coming year*. On a scale from 1 to 10 where 1 means *it's not at all likely* and 10 means *it's very likely*, how likely do you think it is that you will . . .

1. Be approached on the street by a beggar or panhandler?
2. Be cheated, conned or swindled out of your money?
3. Have someone attempt to break into your home while you are away? (Questions 4-10 are the same victimizations as used for the fear of crime items.) Parallel indexes were created for the risk indicators. Alpha for the general risk index is .87; alpha values for personal and property risk indexes are .87 and .77, respectively.

see Tables C–1 and C–2). Next, reliability analyses (based on additive indexes) and factor analyses of the batteries of perceived fear and risk of crime were performed. The factor analyses used both ordinary least squares and maximum-likelihood procedures, but only the latter are presented here—derived from LISREL (Joreskog and Sorbom 1988).

As shown in Table 3–3, Cronbach's alpha coefficients of reliability were computed for the overall indexes of fear and risk of crime as well as subindexes of the items designated as personal offenses and property offenses. To begin, the overall indexes for fear of crime and risk of crime have fairly high reliability; the Cronbach's alpha values are .90 and .87 respectively. Thus, the ten-item indexes are quite consistent in measuring the respective domains.

The subindexes include the item on "burglary while at home" in the personal subindex for both fear and risk. While it is widely considered a property crime, burglary while the resident is present in the dwelling clearly evokes a different set of responses. As will be explained later, a factor analysis suggested this form of the subindex. Several other subindexes were also tested, but these specifications have fairly high reliabilities (see Table 3–3).

Factor analyses based on ordinary least squares (OLS) were used to examine one-factor, two-factor, and three-factor solutions on both the fear and risk indicators (Kim and Mueller 1978). These exploratory analyses showed the value of applying a two-factor approach for what may be considered personal and property crimes. Nevertheless, confirmatory factor analysis was used to test the models identified by OLS methods with alternative measurement models.[7]

Table 3–4 presents the results of the LISREL measurement modeling for fear of crime, with parallel results for risk of crime. As can be seen for fear of crime, only nine of the ten items are used for the final analysis. Models including the item for "being approached on the street by a beggar or panhandler" were inferior in terms of goodness-of-fit. The OLS factor analysis included this item under the property crime factor. In theoretical terms, the item is an example of a public order crime and is probably best not considered as either a personal or property crime. While a three-factor model was estimated to consider this item, it seemed reasonable on the grounds of both goodness-of-fit and parsimony to retain the two-factor model.

A number of alternative models were tested before selecting the models displayed. In sequentially specifying alternative models, it became apparent that the item concerning being robbed/

Table 3–4
LISREL Measurement Model for Perceived Risk and Fear of Crime

	Factor Loadings	
FEAR ITEMS[a]	Personal Crime	Property Crime
1. Burglary/Home	.773	
2. Sexual Assault	.796	
3. Murder	.868	
4. Attack	.942	
5. Cheat/Con		.616
6. Burglary/Away		.742
7. Car Theft		.602
8. Robbery/Mugging	.589	.841
9. Vandalism		.662
RISK ITEMS[b]		
1. Burglary/Home	.720	
2. Sexual Assault	.761	
3. Murder	.805	
4. Attack	.819	
5. Cheat/Con		.447
6. Burglary/Away		.703
7. Car Theft		.643
8. Robbery/Mugging	.594	.799
9. Vandalism		.651

[a]X^2 = 18.79, df = 12, Adjusted goodness-of-fit index = .995. Thirteen of the thirty-six elements on the off-diagonal of the theta epsilon matrix have significant effects (p < .05).
[b]X^2 = 19.09, df = 13, Adjusted goodness-of-fit index = .994. Eleven of the thirty-six elements on the off-diagonal of the theta epsilon matrix have significant effects (p < .05).

mugged (#8) is probably seen by respondents as both a property crime and a personal crime in assessing their fear. Criminologists have long noted the difficulty of classifying some victimizations as either personal or property crimes. By considering it as both, this model yields a much better fit.

The same pattern emerged in the confirmatory factor model for risk of crime. Whereas the OLS exploratory factor pattern of risk differed from the fear factor pattern, no such inconsistency is evident in the LISREL analysis. Again, being robbed or mugged (#8) is considered both a personal and property victimization as respondents assess their risk of crime.[8]

In summary, the additive index, subindexes, and factor analyses of the batteries of separate victimizations all show that these items are useful in assessing fear and risk of crime. As additive indexes, they show very high levels of reliability. The LISREL models show excellent fit to the data. Depending upon one's purpose, these questions can be used by other researchers in the form of additive indexes or subindexes, or as factor-weighted variables. Most importantly, they enable a researcher to distinguish between *types* of crime when assessing a person's perceptions of crime.

THE LINK TO THE UNIFORM CRIME REPORTS

While the survey data were collected confidentially by telephone—no names were obtained—each respondent was asked to identify his or her zip code "to help us make comparisons among the groups of people we have talked to" (Ferraro et al. 1990). By asking zip codes and having telephone numbers as a cross-checking mechanism, we were able to reliably identify the state and county of residence for each respondent. Thus, the link to official risk, in the form of county crime rates, was possible for the survey data (Miethe and Lee [1984] also used county crime rates when studying the state of Washington). The national estimates of crime for the counties were acquired from what are widely known as the *Uniform Crime Reports* (UCR; Federal Bureau of Investigation 1989). Although both "offenses known to the police" and arrest rates are available, the former are used here as the more reliable measures of actual crime prevalence (during 1989, the year before the survey data were collected). Offenses known to the police are generally seen as an underestimate of crime but the rank order for prevalence of types of crime compares favorably to that found in victimization surveys. The same cannot be said about arrest data. Although the UCR data are not perfect estimates of actual risk, they are *official risk* and have been used by most investigators in previous studies as the best available measures of risk (Gove, Hughes, and Geerken 1985; Nettler 1974).

The stage is now set to begin testing the risk interpretation model. No other study has used national data on official and perceived risk for so many types of crime but previous researchers have called precisely for including measures of actual risk in the study of fear (Smith and Hill 1991). Moreover, we have seen that the measures of perceived risk and fear of crime are both psychometrically sound and useful for analysis in several forms. Before turning to a test of the full risk interpretation model, it may be useful to first consider part of the puzzle—how people come to assess their risk of victimization.

CHAPTER 4

Official and Perceived Victimization Risk

It's not the people in prison who worry me. It's the people who aren't.

Earl of Arran (Arthur Gore)

Judging one's risk of criminal victimization is not a simple matter in modern societies, especially in the United States. This is because victimization varies widely in the U.S. and has changed dramatically over time. Moreover the patterns of variation are not always consistent across various types of crime. In this chapter, I briefly review crime prevalence in the United States and then focus on how people come to assess their risk of victimization. Actual crime prevalence should correlate with risk perceptions but other factors from our theoretical model should also shape perceived risk.

CRIME IN THE USA

Although my focus is not explicitly on change in crime over time, it may be useful to start with a terse consideration of how crime rates have changed over the past decades. This may prove helpful for understanding current realities as well as how people may contextualize the crime problem over time. Indeed, most Americans report that crime is a significant and enduring problem but also one that continues to grow (Brantingham et al. 1986; Hindelang et al. 1978).

Figure 4-1 summarizes the change in violent crime from 1960 to 1990 as compiled from the *Uniform Crime Reports* (UCR). (Keep in mind that the UCR measure crimes known to the police. Thus, the UCR are widely seen as an underestimate of the true volume of crime but fairly reliable for identifying the prevalence of types of crime [Nettler 1974].) Figure 4-2 is a parallel graph of

41

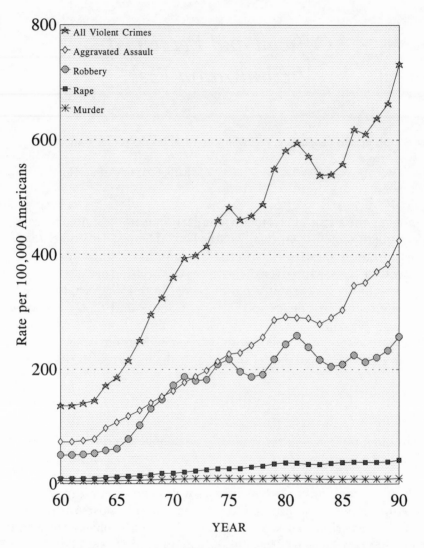

Figure 4–1
Violent Crime Rate in the United States, 1960–1990
Source: Federal Bureau of Investigation 1960–1990, Uniform Crime Reports.

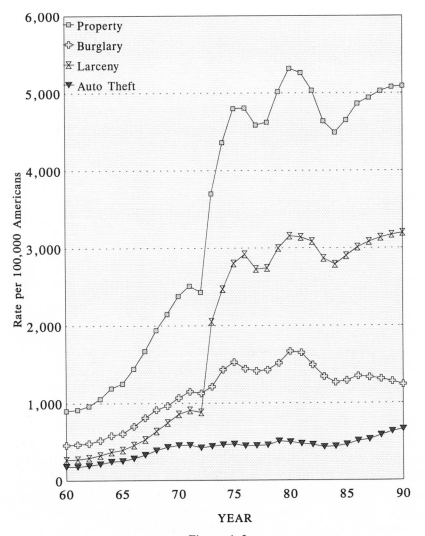

Figure 4–2
Property Crime Rate in the United States, 1960–1990
Source: Federal Bureau of Investigation 1960–1990, *Uniform Crime Reports.*

property crime from 1960 to 1990. It is quite clear that crime soared between 1965 and 1974. Both property and violent (or often called personal) crime rates showed sharp increases during that period but the rate of increase fell after that time. There have been subsequent periodic decreases in rates for some types of crime, especially during the early 1980s. From 1984, however, virtually all types of crime covered in the UCR have continued to increase, although not at nearly the rate of increase seen in the late 1960s and early 1970s (Federal Bureau of Investigation 1990, 1989). The only exception to this is burglary which peaked in 1980; still, the 1990 burglary rate was more than two and one-half times that reported in 1960.

Crime prevalence also varies by location; it is much more likely to occur in large urban areas than in rural areas. Violent crime is about four times more likely in urban areas while property crime is about three times more likely in urban than in rural areas (Federal Bureau of Investigation 1990). As shown in Figure 4-3, the western and southern regions of the U.S. generally rank higher for both violent and property offenses than other regions of the country. The midwest generally has the lowest rates of violent crime while the northeast has the lowest rates of property crime (U.S. Federal Bureau of Investigation 1990). Beyond these basic geographic indicators, crime varies within these areas by traits identified by incivility and routine activity theories (Cohen and Felson 1979; Wilson and Kelling 1982).

As portrayed in media accounts, no segment of society seems immune to the crime plague, although some segments are hit especially hard. Over the life course, virtually every American will become a victim of personal theft, but victimization due to the more serious forms of crime is relatively rare (Bureau of Justice Statistics 1989, 1991; Karmen 1991).[1] There is ample evidence, nonetheless, that crime impels people to be cognizant of it in daily activities and that it is capable of sparking serious psychological concerns (Hindelang et al. 1978; Skogan 1990).

ASSESSING CRIME RISK

People typically estimate their risk of crime with limited information. They rely on the media and "secondhand sources" as well as personal experiences in developing their perceptions of crime (Tyler

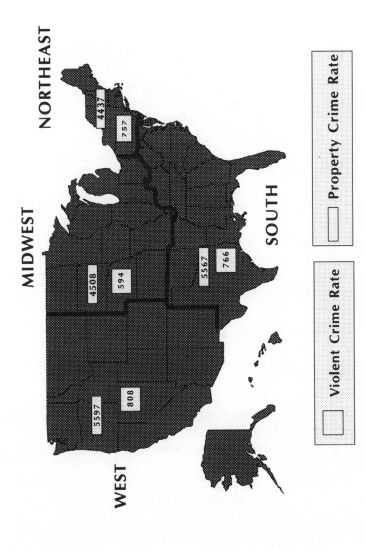

Figure 4-3
Regional Violent and Property Crime Rates 1990 (per 100,000 inhabitants)
Source: Federal Bureau of Investigation 1990, *Uniform Crime Reports*.

and Cook 1984). As such, actors use information from the physical and cultural environment to judge their risk of victimization. Most research comparing crime rates with public estimates of risk reflects a pattern of considerable public accuracy in judging general crime risk at one point in time (Furstenberg 1971; Kleinman & David 1973; Lewis & Salem 1986; McPherson 1978; Stafford & Galle 1984; Warr 1980, 1982).[2] When crime *trends* are considered, most studies report less accuracy; people tend to believe that crime is rising quickly in the nation, is rising less rapidly in their own city than the rest of the country, but is stable in their own neighborhood—what Hindelang et al. (1978) refer to as "crime-is-rising-at-a-distance" phenomenon (see also, Brantingham et al. 1986; Conklin 1975; LaGory & Pipken 1981; U.S. Department of Justice 1977). In short, public estimates of personal crime risk, in the respondent's area and at a given time, correlate quite well with official crime statistics—but the public is less accurate in judging property crime risk, change in crime, and crime prevalence for areas outside of their arena of routine activities.

Part of the reason that public estimates of crime are only moderately related to actual crime risk is that most people attempt to maintain a "perceptual distance" from crime (Hindelang et al. 1978); this is usually reflected in three ways. First, the identities of offenders are most often considered "outsiders" and/or "strangers." Second, routine activities help people place a perceptual distance between themselves and the feelings that they are not safe. People feel safer walking or commuting in *familiar* areas rather than in strange or novel ones (Warr 1990). Their own neighborhoods are often believed to be safer than other areas, regardless of the facts (Pyle 1990). Third, the distinction between "self" and "other" referents means that people generally know that accidents, diseases, and crimes will affect the population but they usually view these events as happening to others (Ferraro 1992; Hedley 1986).[3]

Not only do people often maintain a perceptual distance from crime, but they may also use other information about crime to judge their risk. For instance, while violent crime rates have risen much more slowly in the past decade than in the decade before it, many scholars believe concern about and fear of crime have soared in the more recent period. Actually, we do not have good information on change in fear of crime in the United States during the past two decades.[4] Available evidence, however, suggests that other features of crime, beyond raw rates, may influence people's perceptions. Again, violent crime is rising slowly but the use of guns while committing a crime is rising rapidly—there is evidence that criminals are increasingly likely to be armed with guns. Offenses committed with pistols and revolvers rose from 9.2 percent in 1979 to 12.7 percent in 1992 (*Journal and Courier* 1994). Thus, perceptions of crime may be influenced not only by the prevalence of crime but also by changes in the way crimes are committed. Along this same line, some may argue that the way so many crimes are committed nowadays is exceedingly horrific (Colson 1993).[5]

Table 4-1 shows the rank order of official criminal risk and perceived risk for the six index crimes available in both data sources among respondents of the Fear of Crime in America survey. The official column refers to the UCR rate for the county of the respondents while perceived risk refers to the social survey responses. These data confirm several previous studies and highlight several points. Note first that the rankings for official and perceived risk are identical with the exception of the inversion of items 3 and 4. Most people are aware of their higher risk of property crime victimization, especially for burglary and auto theft, but the most serious crimes of murder and rape rank the lowest for both official and perceived risk. In short, people are generally aware of the relative risk of various types of crime in their areas, and this is reflected in their perceptions of victimization risk.

Table 4–1
Rank Order of Victimization Risk[a]

	Official	*Perceived*
1.	Burglary	Burglary[b]
2.	Auto theft[c]	Auto theft
3.	Assault	Robbery
4.	Robbery	Assault
5.	Rape	Rape
6.	Murder	Murder

[a]Rank order based on comparison of means.
[b]Burglary item for "break into home while away."
[c]Auto theft includes all motor vehicles.

Beyond this simple comparison of ranks, on the basis of risk interpretation theory we would expect that other variables reflecting ecological, neighborhood, and personal characteristics would affect a person's perception of risk. Ecological characteristics specified in the model include the official crime rate for the counties, which can be used as the overall rate and rates for personal and property risk.[6] Other ecological characteristics include region (defined as in the UCR) and urban location. Table C–3 presents the operational definitions of all the ecological as well as the neighborhood and personal characteristics used in the risk interpretation model (see Appendix C: Supplementary Tables).

Neighborhood characteristics include incivility based on nine items covering physical and social incivility as well as neighborhood cohesion based upon three items. Confirmatory factor analysis was used to determine the measurement structure for these two constructs. Crime watch is another neighborhood characteristic signifying the presence or absence of a crime watch program in the respondent's neighborhood.

Personal factors include age, gender, race, education, health (self-assessed), housing tenure, and two measures of victimization. The first indicates that the respondent was victimized in the previous year. Indirect victimization represents whether a family member or close friend was victimized in the previous year.

Table 4-2 presents the results of three equations predicting perceived risk. The first outcome (in column one) is the simple additive index of perceived risk. Personal and property risk refer to the latent variables identified in chapter 3 using confirmatory factor analysis. Turning first to the overall measure of risk, higher perceived risk is found in communities with higher official crime rates as well as in the south and northeast. The only neighborhood variable to influence perceived risk is incivility—but note that it has the strongest effect of any of the variables considered (beta = .28). As expected, women and nonwhite respondents report higher levels of perceived risk. A modest negative effect is observed for health on perceived risk, suggesting that people in better health may feel less vulnerable to victimization. People who have lived in their current residence for longer periods of time report lower levels of risk suggesting the value of familiarity and integration in the neighborhood. Both victimization and indirect victimization increase a person's assessment of risk.

The findings of the separate equations for personal and property risk are quite similar to those for the overall index of risk. In all three equations, incivility has the strongest effect indicating that how one judges one's neighborhood is critical to the risk assessment process. Higher perceived risk of personal and property crime is also associated with higher official crime, the southern and northeastern regions of the U.S., women, nonwhites, and those reporting indirect victimization. Note that for the equation for personal risk, both education and health have negative effects on perceived risk. As suggested earlier, the health effect may indicate that people in better health may feel less vulnerable to crime because they may think they appear as a less suitable target. The fact that health affects personal risk but not property risk strengthens this interpretation.

Direct victimization does not affect perceived risk of personal crime but it has the second largest effect on perceived risk of property crime. As might be expected, the model does a better job predicting perceived risk of property crime than personal crime (i.e., R^2 for personal risk is .19 while the R^2 for property risk is .27). Personal or violent crime is often so erratic or impulsive while property crime is generally more intentional and perhaps predictable (Crutchfield, Geerken, and Gove 1983; Stark 1992). Indeed, the higher value of explained variance (R^2) for property risk confirms this point.

In general, the results show that perceptions of victimization risk correlate with official statistics on the prevalence of crime in an area. The rank ordering of victimizations for official and perceived risk are also very similar. Despite the correlation between official risk and perceived risk, these data provide evidence of how other ecological, neighborhood, and personal characteristics affect perceptions of victimization risk. Respondents from the south and northeast differ from those in the midwest by having higher rates of perceived risk. Respondents from western states face higher prevalence of crime as shown in UCR population data and in the UCR sample data linked here to the survey respondents. Yet, respondents from the western states did not differ significantly from midwesterners on perceived risk once other variables were controlled. This is an intriguing finding worthy of further investigation. In examining the simple relationship between region and perceived risk, respondents from the western states score higher than those from the midwest on all three measures.

Table 4–2
Predicting Perceived Risk of Crime

Independent Variables	Risk	Personal Risk	Property Risk
ECOLOGICAL			
Official Crime	.00[a]**	.00*	.00**
	.10[b]	.08	.08
South[c]	2.44**	.63**	.37*
	.11	.10	.07
West	.85	.29	.12
	.03	.04	.02
Northeast	2.36**	.53*	.40*
	.10	.07	.07
Urban	.64	.23	.26
	.02	.03	.04
NEIGHBORHOOD			
Incivility	2.30**	.60**	.65**
	.28	.25	.34
Cohesion	.09	.02	.04
	.01	.01	.02
Crime Watch	-1.05	-.36	-.21
	-.03	-.04	-.03
PERSONAL			
Age	.01	.00	-.00
	.02	.01	-.01
Gender (women)	3.36**	1.16**	.42**
	.17	.19	.09
Race (nonwhite)	3.52**	1.16**	.46**
	.13	.14	.07
Education	-.46	-.19*	-.02
	-.05	-.07	-.01

Independent Variables	Risk	Personal Risk	Property Risk
Health	-.79*	-.30*	-.17
	-.06	-.07	-.05
Housing Tenure	-.46*	-.13	-.10
	-.07	-.07	-.06
Victimization	2.27**	.11	1.12**
	.09	.02	.19
Indirect Victimization	2.08**	.40*	.56**
	.10	.06	.11
Intercept	18.23	1.04	.09
R^2	.23	.19	.27

[a]Unstandardized coefficient.
[b]Standardized coefficient.
[c]Midwest serves as the reference group for the regional comparisons.
*p ≤ .05.
**p ≤ .01.

When one controls for official crime and the other variables in the model, however, only those in the south and northeast manifest higher perceived risk.

Whether one considers crime in general or personal and property crimes, the single most important predictor of perceived risk is neighborhood incivility. Signs of social and physical incivility such as disruptive neighbors, unsupervised youth, vacant houses, and unkept lots are generally associated with higher perceived crime risk. These phenomena are signals to residents that more vigilance is needed to avoid crime in their daily activities, regardless of how long they have lived in the neighborhood. These results lend considerable support to the "broken windows" thesis when predicting perceived risk.

Personal characteristics are also important in the calculus of risk assessments. Perceived risk is appreciably higher for women and those who are aware of the victimization of significant others. Direct victimization heightens crime perceptions generally but this is especially so for property crime. Given that minority households are more likely to be victimized (Bureau of Justice Statistics 1991), it is not surprising that they also report higher levels of perceived risk. Finally, it should be noted that respondents' average (mean) levels of risk ranged from 2.1 for murder to 4.1 for being approached by a beggar or panhandler. Recalling that the scale for response was 1 to 10, respondents generally feel that incidence of crime is less than 50 percent, but this varies according to the type of crime. Respondents seem quite aware of the different risks associated with various crimes.

The risk interpretation process is affected by macro ecological, neighborhood, and personal characteristics. Each of the three domains is important for judging victimization risk. Our next task is to ask how important risk is to generating fear reactions. We will also want to know whether the same ecological, neighborhood, and personal characteristics also influence fear. The aim is to test the theoretical model of fear of crime specified earlier.

CHAPTER 5

Hitting Paydirt with Risk Interpretation?

Knowledge is the antidote of fear.
Ralph Waldo Emerson

Consider the following illustrations of criminal victimization in modern society.[1]

- A 36-year old Methodist pastor in North Salem, Indiana, was finishing his Sunday morning sermon when he was interrupted by a woman who wanted to speak to him. The pastor had once dated the woman years before, and he asked her to wait until he concluded the sermon. She waited for him to finish and then drew a .38-caliber gun and shot him three times in the chest. He died en route to the hospital.

- Steve, the owner of a custom t-shirt shop felt it was the least he could do. He was troubled about the sexual assaults of young women in the university town in which his shop was located. Therefore, Steve printed dozens of t-shirts bearing the composite of a man police believed was responsible for more than a dozen attacks on women in the past year. He freely distributed the t-shirts to local bars in an attempt to prevent further victimization.

- A 32-year-old black stock brokerage clerk from New York was a tourist in Florida on New Year's Day. He was abducted, driven to a remote area, doused with gasoline, and set on fire. His white assailants taunted him with racial slurs as they watched him burn.

All three illustrations provide information regarding victimization risk in modern America and may shape the way people

53

think about crime. Interpreting victimization risk is a part of our lives, and even when we feel we have taken the adequate precautions to prevent it, victimization forces its way back into our consciousness, whether it be directly or vicariously. Despite the high crime rates in America, the actual frequency of victimization is a tiny fraction of potential crime. Thus, while we hear daily "crime news," we are not all in the same situations as those cited above. Therefore, a person may view *his* or *her* risk of crime, especially violent crime, as quite distinct from the tragic occurences that strike *others*—the crime-at-a-distance phenomenon (Hindelang et al. 1978).

A central thesis of my previous work with Randy LaGrange has been that it is necessary to distinguish between perceived risk and fear in assessing how people feel about criminal victimization (e.g., Ferraro and LaGrange 1987, 1988). Again, we may hear about all kinds of horrific crimes but if they are committed outside our daily sphere of activity, they may not be consequential to our fear of crime. In this work, I have argued that how people interpet their victimization risk is pivotal to understanding why some people are or are not afraid of crime. I now examine this assertion more closely by testing a comprehensive model of fear of crime based on risk interpretation theory, to determine if objective or "official" risk (i.e., crimes known to the police) and perceived risk make much actual difference when trying to explain fear of crime. The focal questions are twofold: What is the relationship between risk and fear? Do people who perceive their risk as high also report high levels of fear? As we will see below, however, answering these questions demands that we attend to other questions as well.

THE RELATIONSHIP BETWEEN RISK AND FEAR

We know that fear is not a knee-jerk reaction where high levels of perceived risk *determine* fear. Stated differently, perceived risk is a necessary but not a sufficient cause of fear. People act in light of their available resources and how they define the situation; therefore, perceptions of risk may precipitate other reactions besides fear. If one perceives that there is risk of a specific victimization, there are at least two likely reactions according to the risk interpretation model of fear of crime stated earlier. Of course, one reaction is fear. The second does not necessarily involve fear—but a decision to constrain behavior on the basis of perceived risk. People can adjust their routine activities ostensibly to lower their chances of victimization risk, although doing so may also affect fear as well.

I refer to such adaptations in one's lifestyle because of the perceived risk of victimization in daily activities as *constrained behavior*. The concept focuses on what people *do*, not just what they think or feel, when they judge their risk of victimization to be high. When studying the relationship between perceived risk and fear, it is critical to simultaneously consider the effects of constrained behavior. Failure to do so could lead to misleading interpretations about the relationship between perceived risk and fear by not accounting for what people *do* when risk is perceived to be high. In other words, perceived risk should affect not only what people feel (i.e., fear) but also what they do (i.e., constrained behavior). While the relationship between beliefs and actions is often complex (Deutscher 1973), social scientists studying crime reactions should include measures of adaptive behavior whenever possible to aid our understanding of how *actors* interpret reality. From an interactionist perspective, it is as people act and interact that definitions of the situation emerge and are revised (Thomas and Thomas 1928).

Constrained behavior has often been measured in previous research by determining if people do things such as install security devices, avoid public transportation, or change their daily activities because of crime (Liska et al. 1988; Taylor et al. 1986). Including constrained behavior in the study of fear of crime was an important contribution for research on this subject, and Taylor et al. and Liska et al. are to be commended for doing so. There are dozens of studies of fear of crime yet so few that go beyond just reporting correlates of fear or purported fear of crime. Unfortunately, the evidence about how constrained behavior affects fear is still an open question. Previous research suggests that constrained behavior may raise fear as suggested by Liska et al. (1988), lower fear, or not even affect fear as reported by Taylor et al. (1986). Given the contradictory findings offered by others and the problems that both of those studies present in measuring fear, the relationships between perceived risk, constrained behavior, and fear of victimization merit further attention.[2] In the model developed here, I will examine constrained behavior as a consequence of perceived risk and a possible cause of fear. I will also test the possibility of a reciprocal relationship between constrained behavior and fear.

Measuring Constrained Behavior

The risk interpretation model of crime fear described throughout explicitly includes constrained behavior as one of the reactions to perceived risk (see Figure 2–2 for a summary of the model). Before testing the relationships among perceived risk, constrained behavior, and fear of crime, however, it is necessary to briefly articulate the measurement of constrained behavior. (I have presented operational definitions for all other variables in the risk interpretation model earlier.) The operational definition of constrained behavior used here is based on two domains of the concept identified in previous research: avoidance behavior and defensive behavior. To measure *avoidance behavior*, subjects were asked three questions:

Do you generally avoid unsafe areas during the day because of crime?

Do you avoid unsafe areas during the night because of crime?

Within the past year, have you limited or changed your daily activities because of crime?

Answers of yes or no were solicited, scored one and zero respectively, and an index of avoidance behavior was created. *Defensive behavior* was measured by asking respondents whether or not they had:

Engraved I.D. numbers on your possessions?

Installed extra locks on windows or doors?

Bought a watchdog?

Kept a weapon in your home for protection?

Added outside lighting?

Learned more about self-defense?

Started carrying something to defend yourself?

Answers of yes or no were solicited, scored one and zero respectively, and an index of defensive behavior was created.

These two indexes were then used as indicators of the construct referred to as constrained behavior. A confirmatory factor analysis indeed showed that the latent variable fits the two domains well with the measurement path (i.e., lambda y) equal to .58 for avoidance and .31 for defensive behaviors. With this variable identified, it is now possible to return to our focal question: What is the relationship between risk and fear?

Does Risk Matter?

Earlier I argued that how people interpet their victimization risk is pivotal to understanding why some people are or are not afraid of crime. If this is correct, we should see that official risk and perceived risk actually make a difference in explaining fear of crime, even when differences in constrained behavior and other factors are taken into account. One fairly simple way to approach this hypothesis is to ask if models of fear of crime with risk variables differ much from those without them.

Using a set of hierarchical regression analyses, the overwhelming evidence is that risk, and especially perceived risk, substantially affect predictions of fear. Without including either official or perceived risk, the percent of variation explained ranged from 20 to 26, depending on the fear measure considered. With the risk measures included, however, the explained variation ranged from 37 percent to 43 percent—a major improvement in predictive ability. Table 5-1 presents the results of three equations including the risk measures and the other variables predicting fear of crime.

The equations in Table 5-1 were selected for presentation after several other models were estimated. It may be useful to begin with two points about the specifications for these equations in discussing the results. First, these models obviously include perceived risk and constrained behavior, but also note that a polynomial term for age has been included (age squared). Earlier research suggested the appropriateness of considering a curvilinear relationship between age and fear (this relationship was uncovered on two different national data sets; see LaGrange and Ferraro [1987] and Ferraro and LaGrange [1992]). The initial tests of this quadratic age term suggested the appropriateness of it (a cubed term was tested but found to be nonsignificant). By examining Table 5-1,

Table 5–1
Predicting Fear of Crime

Independent Variables	Fear	Personal Fear	Property Fear
ECOLOGICAL			
Official Crime	-.00[a]*	.00*	-.00
	-.06[b]	.06	-.04
South[c]	-1.77	-.20	-.14
	-.04	-.03	-.02
West	-2.09	-.15	-.10
	-.04	-.02	-.02
Northeast	.92	.14	.25
	.02	.02	.04
Urban	1.94	.45	.16
	.03	.05	.02
NEIGHBORHOOD			
Incivility	-.49	-.09	-.04
	-.03	-.03	-.02
Crime Watch	-.46	-.02	-.12
	-.01	-.00	-.01
PERSONAL			
Age	-.60**	-.09**	-.05*
	-.45	-.45	-.33
Age^2	.01**	.00*	.00*
	.40	.33	.31
Gender (women)	9.58**	1.64**	.53**
	.22	.24	.10
Race (nonwhite)	2.68**	.40	.32
	.04	.04	.04
Education	-1.17*	-.07	-.09
	-.06	-.02	-.04

Independent Variables	Fear	Personal Fear	Property Fear
Health	-.39*	-.09	.01
	-.01	-.02	.00
Housing Tenure	.27	.05	.03
	.02	.02	.02
Victimization	-.41	.16	-.18
	-.01	.02	-.03
Indirect Victimization	2.47	.58**	.27
	.05	.08	.05
Perceived Risk	.65**	.43**	.65**
	.48	.38	.58
Constrained Behavior	4.54**	.79**	.36**
	.15	.16	.10
Intercept	36.53	1.46	1.06
R^2	.42	.37	.43

[a]Unstandardized coefficient.
[b]Standardized coefficient.
[c]Midwest serves as the reference group for the regional comparisons.
*$p \leq .05$.
**$p \leq .01$.

these terms indicate that fear of crime is highest among *younger* people and declines steadily in adulthood until advanced age. It then increases slightly for the oldest respondents. Second, we have omitted the term for neighborhood cohesion from these specifications. We tested the effects of neighborhood cohesion on risk in chapter four and in preliminary models for its effect on fear in this chapter. Seeing that it was nonsignificant in both cases, it seemed reasonable to delete it from the analyses.[3]

When it comes to which type of risk is more important, it is clear from Table 5-1 that perceived risk has the stronger direct effect, with standardized coefficients ranging from .38 in the equation for personal fear to .58 for property fear. Indeed, the direct effects for official crime are much smaller, and its effect on the global fear index is negative. Even when indirect and total effects are calculated, however, perceived risk is the most important determinant of fear of victimization, whether that is fear of property or personal crime or all crimes considered jointly. None of the remaining ecological and neighborhood variables has a significant direct effect on fear. Rather, the strongest predictors of fear reside in the sphere of personal factors.

In addition to the effects of age and perceived risk noted earlier, women consistently report more fear than men, and this is especially the case for personal fear. Global fear is slightly higher for respondents with limited education but race, health, housing tenure, and direct victimization do not directly affect fear. Indirect victimization increases global and personal fear but not property fear. In each case, constrained behavior is associated with higher levels of fear. Again, fear is not just determined by perceived risk but also shaped by behavioral change intended to reduce risk. While this change may reduce perceived risk over time, it does not, however, reduce fear. Performing acts to reduce risk may actually heighten fear. This is not to imply that constraining one's behavior creates fear where there was none—only that it intensifies such feelings if present. Although he was interested in the power of role performances, Berger's (1963, p. 96) eloquent description of how performances shape emotions is germane to the present investigation:

> Roles carry with them both certain actions and the emotions and attitudes that belong to these actions. The professor putting on an act that pretends to wisdom comes to feel wise. The preacher finds himself believing what he preaches . . . In each case, while the emotion or attitude may have been present before the role was taken on, the latter inevitably strengthens what was there before.

I do not assume that constraining one's behavior will automatically spur fear, but it can do precisely that in some cases. The key is whether or not a person senses high victimization risk. If he or she does, then fear is the most likely outcome. High perceived risk may also prompt constraining one's behavior but doing so does not appear to reduce fear, only to add to it. Before extending the conclusions from this analysis, however, it should prove useful to apply linear structural relations to the full model. Doing so will provide a more rigorous analysis of effects and emphasize the process of risk interpretation.

RISK INTERPRETATION:
MODELING REACTIONS TO CRIME

The analysis is completed with maximum likelihood estimation procedures available in LISREL (Joreskog and Sorbom 1988). Turning to this procedure offers several advantages including the estimation of nonrecursive models and the ability to account for correlated errors of measurement among key variables and correlated errors in equations (Hayduk 1987). The model testing process began with the development of the measurement model according to the procedures recommended by Burt (1976). After testing a variety of measurement models, the best fitting model was selected.[4] The full model was subsequently estimated, and parameter estimates for the measurement structure compared favorably to those derived from estimating the measurement model only.

The complete model specifies the ecological and neighborhood characteristics as causes of perceived risk, constrained behavior, and fear of crime. Constrained behavior and fear are the two reactions considered as a result of perceived risk. Figure 5–1 presents the findings from the risk interpretation model; this one was selected from numerous alternatives as the best model. Coefficients for the measurement structure are omitted for ease in presentation (see note 3 for details). Nonsignificant effects were also deleted in developing the trimmed model. In comparison to Table 5–1, several variables were deleted from the model (i.e., binary variables [scored zero and one] for west and crime watch as well as education and health). The proportion of variance not explained for each equation is displayed as the value of Greek letter ψ (Explained variance is equal to $1 - \psi$). Indirect and total effects were also estimated and will be referred to in discussing the results.[5]

Given that others have considered the possibility of reciprocal relations between constrained behavior and fear of crime, several nonrecursive models were also tested. Liska et al. (1988) reported a feedback effect for fear on constrained behavior, and I attempted to replicate such a model. None of the nonrecursive models, using alternative instrumental variables (Heise 1975), showed a significant effect for fear on constrained behavior. Again, Liska et al. (1988) did not consider perceived risk and fear as separate concepts in their research, and this no doubt contrib-

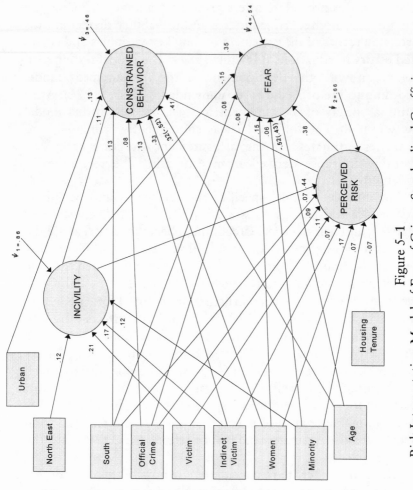

Figure 5–1
Risk Interpretation Model of Fear of Crime: Standardized Coefficients
(Effects of age squared are listed in parentheses)

utes to the lack of replicability; quite simply, the models tested are different (the same is true for comparisons with Taylor et al. 1986).

The model displayed in Figure 5-1 shows that incivility substantially shapes perceived risk which, in turn, has moderately strong effects on both constrained behavior and fear. Of all the variables considered, perceived risk is the strongest predictor of fear followed by constrained behavior. This is not only the case for the direct effects displayed in Figure 5-1 but also for total effects. The total effect of perceived risk on fear is .64 while the total effect of constrained behavior on fear is .52. The strength of effects due to perceived risk is similar to what others report when including it in studies of fear of crime (Bankston and Thompson 1989; Lee 1982a; Miethe and Lee 1984; Riger et al. 1978; Warr 1984).

Similar to what was observed in Table 5-1, the higher one's perceived risk, the more he or she has constrained everyday activities; and the more a person constrains everyday activities, the more fearful of crime he or she will be. One might intuitively think that constraining one's actions would decrease fear but this does not occur—at least not immediately. It is possible that this may transpire over time and that the cross-sectional data used here will not detect such an effect. Whatever the case, the evidence from these data offer limited support to the finding of Liska and others (1988) that constrained behavior is associated with higher fear, although there is no evidence from these data that there is an escalating loop between constrained behavior and fear. Instead, perceived risk shapes constrained behavior which in turn influences fear.

Although incivility strongly and positively affects perceived risk, the direct effect on fear is weak and negative. When calculating total effects, incivility's effect on fear is positive and significant (.12) but not nearly as substantial in comparison to its effect on perceived risk (.36). These results, completed with structural equation modeling, are quite consistent with those presented in LaGrange et al. (1992) using ordinary least squares to show that the effect of incivility on fear is almost entirely mediated through perceived risk of crime. Therefore, to assume that removing the "riffraff" from the streets and cleaning up the vacant buildings will reduce fear of crime is probably an oversimplification. It will help somewhat but other factors also shape fear.

Among the other ecological variables considered, urban residents report higher levels of constrained behavior and, when considering total effects, slightly higher levels of fear. Residents of the northeast report higher levels of incivility while southern residents report higher perceived risk and constrained behavior but slightly lower levels of fear. Official crime positively affects perceived risk and constrained behavior but the direct effect on fear is negative. When one considers total effects, however, official crime is not a significant predictor of fear.

Turning to the personal characteristics, victimization, both direct and indirect, play important roles in the risk interpretation model. Neither has an effect on fear—either direct or total—but both influence perceived risk. Indirect victimization is also associated with higher levels of constrained behavior. Gender has the strongest effects among the personal variables with women reporting higher levels of perceived risk, constrained behavior, and fear. That women have higher levels of fear is consistently reported in the literature (e.g., Lee 1982a; Warr 1984). Chapter 7 provides greater insight into this and related findings and attempts to explain why women have higher fear.

Thinking of fear of crime often conjures up images of minority neighborhoods in large urban centers. It is clear from these data that minority respondents live in neighborhoods with higher levels of official crime ($t = 5.8$, $p < .01$). In an objective sense, they face higher personal and property crime risk in their living environments. It should not be surprising, therefore, that minority respondents are more likely to report living in neighborhoods characterized by high levels of incivility. Even if one controls for incivility and official crime, minorities judge their risk of crime to be higher and are more afraid (these effects are also present when total effects are considered). The overall picture that emerges is of a population which faces higher risk, knows it, and is also afraid of criminal victimization (Ortega and Myles 1987).

When it comes to age differences, the highest levels of fear are found among younger respondents (in contrast to what many investigators have reported). Fear of crime declines over the ages but rises slightly in older adulthood. Just as reported in Table 5–1, the relationship between age and fear of crime is curvilinear, and chapter 6 will probe this relationship in greater detail. Note however, from Figure 5–1, that the relationship between age and constrained behavior is just the opposite as that observed with fear. Constrained behavior is lowest among youth and rises steadily in adulthood until a drop in later life. Recall that constrained behavior is measured by asking people how they changed their behavior due to crime. It may be that older adults have "constrained" their behavior but for other reasons. Especially with regard to avoidance behaviors, older adults may not go out as much—especially at night—because of limitations in vision, driving ability, or social activity not because of crime. Finally, housing tenure is negatively associated with perceived risk. Despite changes in the neighborhood over time, it appears that familiarity with the neighborhood and residing in the same home reduce perceived crime risk (Miethe and Lee 1984).

The explained variance in the equations for perceived risk, constrained behavior, and fear are quite respectable for survey data (.34, .54, and .46 respectively). On the whole, our test of the model leads one to conclude that ecological, neighborhood, and personal characteristics should all be considered when attempting to understand fear of victimization. The ecological and neighborhood variables are most important in shaping perceived risk; most of their effect on fear is indirect. The personal characteristics appear to influence both perceived risk and fear with the relationship between those two being fairly strong. The result of including constrained behavior in the model also shows the importance of what actors do in understanding affectual states. In alternative models omitting constrained behavior, one is less able to explain variation in fear of crime.

Based on these data, I feel that the risk interpretation model is a reasonable depiction of the reality circumscribed within fear of crime—we have hit paydirt. It is nonetheless a model, and one that needs further testing and elaboration. When the overall model was estimated separately for personal and property crime, relationships among the core concepts were very similar although effects for some covariates differed. The basic model needs replication on other national samples and would profit greatly from longitudinal applications. Indeed, panel studies may be the most rigorous way to further study the relationship between constrained behavior and fear. I welcome other investigators to attempt to replicate (or refute) the model. The model assembles much of what we know about the development of fear of crime using ecological and personal variables. If it is robust, including related characteristics should not substantially change the way in which the core concepts are related.

Given the intriguing relationships unveiled between both age and gender and the risk interpretation process, more attention to them seems warranted. In chapter 6, we consider the age relationships and attempt to explain why the findings presented here differ from so many reported in the literature.

CHAPTER 6

Are Older People Prisoners of Fear?

In essence, then, there is solid documentation that the elderly suffer from a substantial fear of crime.

Frank Clemente and Michael Kleiman (1976)

Fear of crime is a less severe problem for the elderly than previous reports suggest.

Peter Yin (1982)

A finding from the last chapter and a vast array of previous articles and books prompt further attention to the question of aging and fear of crime. Indeed, controversy over the prevalence of fear of crime by age is what prompted me to embark on this research program over 10 years ago. The conventional wisdom for at least a decade was that fear of crime is higher among older adults than among younger people (Clemente and Kleiman 1976; Hindelang, Gottfredson, and Garofalo 1978; Jaycox 1978; Lewis and Salem 1986; Lindquist and Duke 1982; Moeller 1989; Ortega and Myles 1987). For example, Ollenburger's (1981, p. 101) analysis of an adult sample of Nebraska residents shows that "the elderly have the highest fear of crime." Her analysis also shows that fear of crime was much stronger among the urban elders than the rural elders. Clemente and Kleiman concluded "Simply put, fear among the elderly is real and pervasive" (1976, p. 208). These and other studies have prompted numerous other investigations which do not compare older and younger persons on fear of crime but examine only variations in the phenomenon among older adults (e.g., Akers et al. 1987; Lee 1982b).

It is apparent in the way that the literature has developed that some researchers have viewed the finding that older people are more afraid of crime than their younger counterparts as axiomatic. Consider the idea of the victimization/fear paradox (Lindquist and Duke 1982). Whereas most crime statistics reveal that younger persons—especially teenagers and young adults—are much more likely to be victimized (Bachman 1992; Liang and Sengstock 1981), the level of fear among older adults is thus considered extraordinarily high (Cook and Cook 1976). In other words, why should older people be so fearful, more than other age groups, when their actual risk of being victimized is quite low? Clemente and Kleiman (1976) go so far in interpreting the victimization-fear paradox as to posit that "it is reasonable to argue that for older people fear of crime is even more of a problem than crime itself" (p. 207).

Adding fuel to this debate regarding the victimization-fear paradox are discussions of the "rationality" of older persons' fear and statements implying that the only thing older people have to fear is fear itself (Jaycox 1978; Lindquist and Duke 1982). As a result, some researchers posit that older adults are irrational in their fear of crime. It is even asserted by some that many older persons are so afraid of crime that they have isolated themselves from the outside world and may be "captives" in their own homes (Braungart, Hoyer, and Braungart 1979; Clemente and Kleiman 1976; Time 1976, 1985).

Some researchers have more recently questioned the conventional wisdom that older adults are highly afraid of crime (Bankston and Thompson 1989; Ferraro and LaGrange 1988; Jeffords 1983; LaGrange and Ferraro 1987, 1989; Lawton and Yaffe 1980; Yin 1980, 1982). The main reason offered for this conclusion by many of these researchers—myself included—hinges on how fear of crime is measured. Peter Yin (1980, 1982, 1988) was one of the first researchers to present compelling data and arguments that older people are not the most fearful age category. If Yin (1982, p. 240) is correct in stating that "fear of crime is a less severe problem for the elderly than previous reports suggest," then American society has been led to hold an inaccurate image of older adults. Elderly people are all too often *expected* to be fearful of crime, which may lead many persons, of all ages, to become concerned about yet another "problem" of growing older. The research questions raised here are not just epistemological but relevant to policy decisions and societal images of the process of growing older. Some of the published results appear to either overestimate or underestimate fear of crime among older adults.

Many older persons are no doubt afraid of crime. The concern of this chapter, however, lies in assessing how prevalent such fear is among various age groups. In the last chapter, we found that the relationship between age and fear of crime is not linear—one cannot just say that as age increases fear of crime decreases or increases. Instead, the relationship between age and fear of crime is more complex. In this chapter, I will try to offer some suggestions as to why other studies yield discrepant findings and then, using our national survey data, describe the relationship between age and fear of crime in more detail.

WHY THE DISCREPANT FINDINGS?

The discrepant findings regarding age differences in fear of crime could be due to a number of reasons. Five possible explanations for the inconsistency in empirical results appear salient: measurement, sampling, data collection methods, analytic methods, and social change. It should be noted that each of these concerns could influence results, let alone the combination of these factors in previous research.

Measurement

First, some investigators argue that the problem of fear of crime among older people has been overestimated because of limitations in defining and *measuring* fear of crime (Ferraro and LaGrange 1987, 1988; LaGrange and Ferraro 1989; Yin 1982). Most of these concerns were previously discussed in chapter 3 but how they affect findings regarding age differences is what I emphasize here. To begin, most studies of age differences in fear of crime are based on single-item indicators of fear. In terms of content validity, can a single-item indicator possibly be representative of the phenomenon of fear of crime, when *crime* entails so many different acts? On the basis of measurement and criminological theory, it seems most unlikely (Kerlinger 1986). Second, as noted earlier, numerous studies use the same indicators from the National Crime Survey (NCS) and the General Social Survey (GSS; see Ferraro and LaGrange 1987, 1988 for reviews). From a methodological viewpoint, there are numerous problems with these measures. Such global, single-item indicators do not differentiate across types of crime and have limited validity; it is also difficult to assess their reliability (Ferraro and LaGrange 1987; Furstenberg 1971; Garofalo 1979).

The NCS and GSS measures can be useful social indicators inasmuch as they have been collected on national samples for several years now. The concern identified here is the interpretation of these measures. Numerous studies use these measures, or very similar indicators, and interpret them as fear of crime (e.g., Moeller 1989).[1] Others have analyzed these same or similar measures and not generalized their findings so directly to fear of crime (e.g., Brillon 1987; Cutler 1980). We collected the NCS and GSS measures in the Fear of Crime in America survey as well as in an earlier pilot study (LaGrange and Ferraro 1989) in an attempt to replicate the age findings reported by others.[2]

In our earlier study of one North Carolina county we found that age was negatively related to crime specific fear indicators (similar but not identical to the ones used here) while age was positively, albeit weakly, related to the NCS measure. In the national survey used throughout this book, age was not found to be significantly related to either of the NCS measures. For the GSS measure, a nonlinear bivariate relationship among men was uncovered; men 18–34 and 50–64 years old were most likely to be afraid to walk alone at night with the other men less likely. In multivariate models, however, this nonlinear age effect was not present. If one considers the magnitude of effects in many of the original studies as well as in our replication of the NCS and GSS measures, one is struck by the trivial size of effects. Some studies rely on percentage differences but even the more recent studies employing multivariate analyses show only trivial effects for age—often explaining less than one percent of the variance (Moeller 1989; Ortega and Myles 1987).

Our earlier work suggested that the NCS measures were probably better indicators of perceived risk than fear (Ferraro and LaGrange 1987; 1988). With the data now in hand, there is evidence for our expectation. Indeed, one of the major findings from the replication exercises is that both the NCS and GSS measures are more strongly related to our index of perceived risk than they are to the fear index (Ferraro and LaGrange 1992). Table C–4 presents the correlations between the additive fear and risk indexes from our survey and the replication measures reflecting this finding. In short, measurement differences alone may not be sufficient to reconcile the literature on age difference in fear of crime. Nevertheless, among the studies which ask about fear of specific victimizations, it appears that older people are not more afraid in most circumstances (e.g., Warr 1984).

Sampling

It is possible that some of the inconsistency in results is due to variation in sampling. There are both national and regional studies which report older people to be most afraid of crime and use measures similar to the GSS or NCS measures—questions which do not differentiate among the types of crime (e.g., Clemente and Kleiman 1976; Ortega and Myles 1987). Most previous studies of fear which differentiate across types of crime are limited to community or state samples (e.g., Bankston et al. 1990; LaGrange and Ferraro 1989; Warr 1984). To date, I believe the present study is the only one to use a national sample to examine age differences in *fear* across the various types of crime (Ferraro and LaGrange 1992). (As will be described later, a 1982 national survey examined *worry* involving different types of crime.)

Data Collection Methods

Another possibility is that various data collection procedures and/ or interviewing effects may influence responses to questions about a sensitive subject such as crime. Most studies showing a positive relationship between age and the NCS or GSS measures have used face-to-face interviewing while a few have used telephone interviews (e.g., Baker et al. 1983). By contrast most surveys which find a negative relationship between age and fear of crime are based on mail questionnaires (e.g., Bankston and Thompson 1989; Jeffords 1983) or telephone interviews (e.g., LaGrange and Ferraro 1989). It is possible that face-to-face interviews may heighten fear of crime reporting for older adults, but this thesis cannot be tested here. Data collection experiments would be needed to test such a thesis.

A related concern is question-order effects (sometimes called context effects). As noted earlier, using our national survey data, we could not replicate the positive relationship between age and the NCS and GSS measures. In our survey instrument, we used the NCS and GSS measures *after* asking the respondents about fear and perceived risk. In a sense, our questions covering the ten victimizations may have yielded different NCS and GSS responses than what one would obtain without such a "funnel" (Frey 1983; Schuman and Presser 1981). Question-order experiments could address this concern in a systematic way.

Analytic Methods

Studies of fear of crime over the last two decades have employed a variety of analytic strategies. Most have been multivariate analyses controlling for gender, race, and some indicator of social class, although numerous possibilities in the way these analyses are conducted can affect findings. Only a few studies have attempted to differentiate fear from risk of crime. Of those that do, the practice most widely adopted is to treat perceived risk as a covariate in the prediction of fear (Stafford and Galle 1984; Warr 1984; Warr and Stafford 1983). Analyses then examine the residuals of fear after being regressed on risk. Failure to control for risk is widespread and is related to the problem of measurement. Most of the studies which show a positive relationship between age and the NCS or GSS measures do not control for either official or perceived risk.

As noted earlier, several studies collect fear items on specific victimizations. Indeed, all studies which do this find that the *age relationships differ across the types of crime*. Nevertheless, one may want to generalize beyond specific crimes. Thus, aggregating victimizations into indexes or factor variables involves numerous psychometric decisions likely to affect findings.

Social Change

Most of the studies reporting a negative relationship between age and fear of crime not only use a battery of victimizations to assess fear but also have been conducted more recently (e.g., Bankston and Thompson 1989; LaGrange and Ferraro 1989). Might it be possible that most of the reported findings are correct and that, because of the social change that occurred, older persons' fear decreased from the early 1970s to the present? Very few studies of social change are available, but Cutler (1980) has shown that fear of walking alone at night (GSS item) *increased* between 1965 and 1976. Ferraro (1992) showed that Americans of all ages, including older persons, felt that the problem of fear of crime became more serious between 1974 and 1981. We do not have social change analyses which cover the late 1980s or early 1990s, but it might be possible that fear of crime increased through the late 1970s and early 1980s and decreased in the last few years. While such a social change thesis may be plausible, there is some evidence that when differentiating among types of crime, the *negative* relationship between age and fear may not be just a recent phenomenon. LaGrange and Ferraro's (1987) reanalysis of a 1982 ABC News Poll shows that *worry* about crime was negatively related to age in four out of seven victimizations considered.

After considering five possible reasons for the discrepant findings on aging and fear of crime, it appears that differences in measurement cannot be ignored. Other design and analysis factors are no doubt important, but differences in measurement need more careful investigation for assessing age differences in fear of crime. The analysis presented below cannot, in and of itself, solve the mystery. It should, however, help us better understand the measurement concerns. It is only as further studies are done, especially longitudinal ones, that we can arrive at a complete understanding of why the discrepant findings exist.

PRISONERS OF FEAR?

Are older adults prisoners of fear of crime? A curvilinear relationship between age and fear was uncovered while testing the risk interpretation model of fear of crime. This means that older adults' fear was higher than people in their 50s. But how much greater? When considering all ages, are older people the age group with the highest fear of crime? And how does their fear compare to younger people (located at the other end of the curve)? To answer these questions, it may be useful to first consider each victimization separately by age and to also use age categories to better demarcate the relationships.

Table 6–1 presents the zero-order correlation coefficients of age, coded in years, and each of the ten items as well as the aforementioned indexes, subindexes, and latent variables (based upon the LISREL analyses). In addition to the simple correlations, the table also presents mean levels of the variables under consideration by four age categories in order to detect any nonlinearities. Although categorizing age is an arbitrary decision, these categories were selected to facilitate comparisons with previous research

Table 6-1
Age Differences in Measures of Fear of Crime by Gender

FEAR ITEMS	Simple Correlation	Age			
		18–34 (N = 368)	35–49 (N = 355)	50–64 (N = 194)	65+ (N = 172)
Burglary/Home	-.14[a]*	6.57	5.84	5.40	5.32
	-.07[b]	4.07	3.73	3.91	3.40
Sexual Assault	-.22*	6.96	6.14	5.54	5.05
	-.10*	2.33	2.29	2.13	1.62
Murder	-.17*	6.12	5.16	4.91	4.48
	-.14*	3.95	3.42	2.74	3.12
Attack	-.15*	6.41	5.56	5.36	5.06
	-.12*	4.62	4.40	3.84	3.76
Beggar	.12*	3.24	3.04	3.26	4.21+
	.08	2.26	2.29	2.49	2.67
Cheat/Con	.00	4.06	3.59	3.61	4.19
	-.13*	3.86	3.16	3.16	2.93
Burglary/Away	-.10*	6.57	6.12	6.23	5.57
	-.02	5.22	5.20	5.27	4.91
Car Theft	-.05	5.18	4.34	4.76	4.77+
	-.07	4.62	3.88	4.14	4.19

Robbery/Mugging	-.14*	5.68	4.94	4.64	4.51
	-.02	3.73	3.60	3.45	3.88
Vandalism	-.04	5.06	4.88	4.78	4.73
	-.02	4.49	4.11	4.36	4.17
FEAR INDEX	-.13*	55.84	49.65	48.50	48.07
	-.10*	39.17	35.99	35.64	34.66
FEAR SUBINDEXES					
Personal	-.19*	26.06	22.66	21.09	20.03
	-.13*	15.00	13.84	12.54	11.90
Property	-.09*	26.54	23.93	24.04	23.73
	-.07	21.92	20.00	20.53	20.09
LATENT VARIABLES					
Personal	-.19*	1.98	1.00	.55	.28
	-.12*	-1.05	-1.37	-1.75	-1.78
Property	-.10*	.88	.25	.25	.16
	-.07	-.30	-.74	-.62	-.71

[a]Women
[b]Men
*p<.05 (correlation of age and item).
+p<.05 (deviation from linearity among age categories).

(e.g., Warr 1984). In addition to this relatively simple four-category breakdown, subsequent analyses will examine a seven-category classification. Tests for deviations from linearity were also performed.

Sex-specific statistics are presented here for two reasons. First, the literature is quite consistent in showing that sex differences in fear of crime are substantial—women are more afraid. (The findings presented in the last chapter confirm the importance of sex differences in understanding fear of crime; presenting sex-specific statistics should help to uncover some of the differences and serve as a bridge to chapter 7.) Second, sex differences in mortality mean that older populations are disproportionately female. Presenting the data by sex permits one to examine variation both within and between each sex. Because of the salience of the concept, Table 6-2 presents these correlations with the risk of crime indicators.

Examining the findings of Table 6-1 reveals that in three out of ten instances, the simple correlation between the individual fear items and age is significant and *negative* for both women and men. For an additional three offenses, the simple correlation with age is significant and negative for women only. For women, only the correlation between fear of being approached by a beggar and age is significant and positive. Tests for deviations from linearity between the age categories and fear reveal significant nonlinearities for only two items. The questions for beggar and car theft both show a nonlinear relationship. The relationship between age and the beggar item is j-shaped, meaning that older women have the highest level of fear and women 35–49 the lowest level, with the other categories in between. The pattern for car theft is reverse j-shaped—youngest women are most afraid.

The correlation for the overall additive fear index is negative for both women (-.13) and men (-.10). This same basic pattern is observed for the personal subindex and the latent variable for personal fear, but the negative relationship between age and fear of property crime is significant only for women with the subindex and the latent variable.

Table 6-2 shows that for the perceived risk questions on burglary/home, sexual assault, beggar, cheat/con, and vandalism, the simple correlations with age are significant and *negative* for women. A significant negative correlation is also present for the cheat/con and vandalism items for men. In no instance is the correlation between age and any risk variable significant and positive. All of the risk indexes and latent variables are negatively related to age for women. For men, the only significant effects are observed between age and the overall risk index and between age and the property risk subindex. There are no significant nonlinear relationships by age with any of the risk measures. Thus, perceived risk is quite congruent with official crime statistics by age— older adults even judge their risk of victimization accurately.

To probe the relationships between age and the types of crime even further, age was next categorized into seven intervals (ten years for most categories). Means for each age group were then tested with multiple classification analysis to further assess the possibility of nonlinear effects. If nonlinear effects are observable, especially on the constructed variables, then it would be wise for future research to use dummy variables for each age group and/or perhaps polynomial terms for age. Official and perceived risk of crime measures corresponding to each fear of crime variable will be used as a covariate in assessing these age differences following the procedures of others (Stafford and Galle 1984; Warr 1984).[3]

Nonlinearities in the relationship between age and fear of crime in these models are readily anticipated. As LaGrange and Ferraro (1987) point out with national data, the relationship between age and fear of some crimes may be curvilinear—often reverse J-shaped. Figure 6–1 presents the results of a multiple classification analysis of three fear-of-crime variables: the additive index from ten items as well as the latent variables (estimated by LISREL) for personal fear and property fear. When breaking age down into seven categories, one finds that the fear of crime index is lowest for those aged 55–64 and highest for those aged 18–24. Senior citizens, those 65–74 and 75+, have slightly higher levels than respondents 55–64; yet the means for the two oldest categories (43.3 and 43.7 respectively) are lower than the grand mean for the entire sample (44.5). In other words, *older adults have lower than average fear.* What is striking is the extraordinarily high level of fear among those 18–24, even though we are controlling for official and perceived risk of crime in the analysis.

A very similar pattern to what was discovered for the entire additive index exists for the analysis of the latent variable for fear of personal crime. For fear of property crime, the youngest age category again shows the highest level of fear, and the 75+ category manifests the *lowest* level of fear. The age differences among

Table 6–2
Age Differences in Perceived Risk of Crime by Gender

RISK ITEMS	Simple Correlation	Age			
		18–34 (N = 368)	35–49 (N = 355)	50–64 (N = 194)	65+ (N = 172)
Burglary/Home	-.09a*	2.94	2.89	2.58	2.50
	-.01b	2.12	1.99	2.12	2.03
Sexual Assault	-.16*	3.41	3.12	2.41	2.51
	.02	1.28	1.49	1.36	1.43
Murder	-.01	2.26	2.29	1.95	2.36
	-.02	1.83	1.86	1.60	1.79
Attack	-.06	2.97	2.71	2.33	2.71
	-.07	2.53	2.33	2.30	2.12
Beggar	-.15*	4.14	4.30	3.30	2.84
	-.09	4.86	4.51	4.64	3.47
Cheat/Con	-.13*	4.06	3.70	3.03	3.12
	-.17*	4.62	4.01	3.66	3.17
Burglary/Away	-.07	4.31	4.31	4.16	3.73
	-.05	3.87	3.48	3.53	3.38

Car Theft	a	-.06	4.09	3.69	3.64	3.53
	b	-.02	3.87	3.25	3.60	3.72
Robbery/Mugging	a	-.07	3.44	3.31	2.58	3.14
	b	.07	2.71	2.42	2.74	3.02
Vandalism	a	-.14*	4.21	3.70	3.53	3.05
	b	-.16*	3.88	3.15	3.01	2.84
RISK INDEX	a	-.14*	35.81	34.24	29.44	29.57
	b	-.09*	31.37	28.27	28.10	27.43
RISK SUBINDEXES						
Personal	a	-.09*	11.59	11.05	9.27	10.07
	b	-.04	7.76	7.69	7.20	7.41
Property	a	-.13*	26.10	18.77	16.93	16.51
	b	-.11*	18.75	16.17	16.32	16.14
LATENT VARIABLES						
Personal	a	-.09*	.97	.73	-.15	-.32
	b	-.01	-.67	-.78	-.89	-.71
Property	a	-.12*	.59	.28	-.20	-.29
	b	-.08	.10	-.53	-.42	-.40

aWomen.
bMen.
*p < .05 (correlation of age and item).

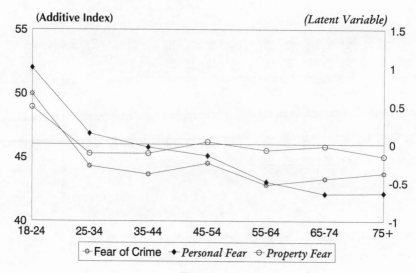

Figure 6–1
Adjusted Means for Fear of Crime by Age:
Multiple Classification Analysis

people 25 years and older are modest. The major age difference in all three equations is the very high level of fear among those 18–24 years of age. Indeed, in supplementary analyses excluding the 18–24 age bracket, the main effects for the remaining age categories are nonsignificant in all three equations. The age group 55–64 also has consistently low levels of fear of crime. Just as shown in chapter 5, regression-based models with polynomial terms for age (age and age squared) were found to be preferable to model the relationship between age and fear of crime. It is recommended from these analyses that future researchers explicitly consider the possibility of curvilinear effects between age and fear of crime.

VICTIMS OF ANOTHER KIND?

The title of this chapter explicitly asks one question and poses several others in an implicit fashion. To answer the overarching research question, no—older people are not prisoners of fear of crime. Indeed, they are generally less likely than younger people to be afraid of crime. When examining the ten victimizations, it was discovered that younger people were more afraid of several types of crime including burglary while at home, burglary while away, sexual assault, murder, attack, and robbery/mugging. For other crimes, there was no significant relationship with age (i.e., car theft, vandalism). The only instance in which older people showed higher levels of fear than younger people was fear of being approached on the street by a beggar or panhandler, and this relationship was only significant among the women in this sample. In all analyses involving indexes and the latent variables of fear, older adults were not found to be the most afraid. Rather, younger persons reported greater fear than older persons for these analyses.

Using both multiple classification analysis and polynomial regression, nonlinearity in the relationship between the overall index and age was detected. Age was negatively related to the fear index, but the oldest members of the sample showed a slight reversal of this trend. In short, even the oldest (75+) respondents' fear was lower than that of the youngest adults in this sample, although it was slightly higher than people aged 50–64. The relationship could best be described as reverse j-shaped.

Given the variety of methods and strategies used to detect age effects, one conclusion from these data is inescapable: older people are not any more likely to be fearful of crime than are other age groups. It appears from these data that many previous studies have exaggerated the prevalence of fear of crime among older people (e.g., Braungart, Braungart, and Hoyer 1980; Clemente and Kleiman 1976; Janson and Ryder 1983; Lindquist and Duke 1982; Mullen and Donnermeyer 1985). While one cannot be absolutely certain as to why so many of the previous studies show older people to be so fearful, it is suspected that the measures used to assess fear of crime are of questionable validity, especially because they do not differentiate between the types of crime. Warr's (1984) analysis of fear across crime types found that in eleven of sixteen victimizations, there were no significant age differences. Only two of the five that were significant in Warr's research were asked in this survey, and the findings here replicate those which he reported. Further research is needed on how questions are worded and which offenses are included to better understand why findings from these surveys may differ. I welcome others to attempt to replicate these findings or to experiment with sets of offenses which may likely spark fear responses among older adults. It may be that forcing respondents to assess fear at night, like the NCS and GSS items do, may increase older adults' fear (Warr 1990). We see limited value, however, in further promoting research on fear of crime which uses only single-item indicators of fear, especially fear at night.

Older adults are not any more likely than younger adults to rate their risk of crime higher. Although the simple correlations indicate that older women and men are more likely to estimate their risk to be low for both the overall risk index and the property subindex, the age difference disappears once one controls for gender and community characteristics. Based on what we know about actual victimization rates, older adults do not even judge their risk of crime inaccurately (Warr 1982). Although some researchers have suggested that older adults are inaccurate in judging crime relative to other age groups, the present research finds no evidence for this proposition.

If one chooses to characterize age differences in fear of crime as important, these analyses show that younger people are the age group most afraid. Consider when most crime is committed, especially violent or personal crime: during the night. Because the GSS and NCS force respondents to report safety or fear at night, those items may trigger higher "fear" among older people. Yet, most older people simply do not engage in the activities mentioned in those questions—walking alone in their neighborhood at night. Indeed, older adults have less need to be out at night for whatever reasons and, therefore, are not as afraid—they probably also realize what behaviors are high risk. It would be helpful to recall that the older population is a *survivor* population. People who engaged in high risk behaviors have a lesser chance of even making it into older ages.

I think that the overwhelming evidence to date shows convincingly that age differences in fear of crime in adulthood are modest to trivial when we consider those people who are 25 years of age or older. Youth and young adults have higher risk and are also more afraid. There really is no victimization/fear paradox by age as described in the literature.

LaGrange and Ferraro (1987) noted that "most Americans—especially those under 65—consider fear of crime a very serious problem for the elderly" (p. 387). While the public and the mass media may think that older people are "prisoners of fear," it appears that relatively few older people are in fact excessively frightened by crime in America. The findings from this research do not support those predicated on the victimization-fear paradox (Lindquist and Duke 1982). Older adults generally have lower rates of criminal victimization (Bachman 1992), perceive their risk as such, and are not the age category most afraid of crime. I feel it is totally unreasonable to "argue that for older people fear of crime is even more of a problem that crime itself" (Clemente and Kleiman 1976, p. 207). Neither older people nor their interpretation of victimization risk are the problem. Crime is. While some elders are no doubt very afraid of crime, Binstock (1983) claims ageism exists when people homogenize the older population on the basis of a stereotypical image. Perhaps the older population has suffered a different type of victimization—a stereotyping of older people by the media and the (younger) public as inaccurate and irrational in assessing crime risk.

If one is interested in finding the status characteristic that most likely affects fear, age is a poor candidate. Sex is a far more substantial predictor and the one to which we now turn our attention.

CHAPTER 7

Unraveling Fear of Crime
Among Women

In grief we know the worst of what we feel, but who can tell the end
of what we fear?

Hannah More

A quite consistent finding from previous research and earlier
chapters is that women are more afraid of crime. Dozens of studies report higher fear of crime among women; these include studies using the National Crime Survey and General Social Survey
indicators (e.g., Lebowitz 1975; Liska et al. 1988) as well as studies with more valid indicators of fear (e.g., Akers et al. 1987; Warr
1984).[1] Virtually all investigations which examine fear across different victimizations show important gender effects for each
offense as well as for overall fear (e.g., Bankston and Thompson
1989; Ferraro and LaGrange 1992; Warr 1984).

As discussed in the previous chapter, when one examines the
magnitude of effects due to status characteristics, gender is consistently the most important predictor—often twice as strong as
other variables. With the dozens of studies directed at older
adults' fear of crime, it is perplexing that, by comparison, so few
investigators have given detailed attention to gender differences
and why they are so strong. Baumer (1978) long ago bemoaned
that "we know who is afraid but very little about why they are
afraid" (p. 254). While there has been important progress in the
study of fear of crime among women since that time, our knowledge about why women are more afraid remains quite modest.
The purpose of this chapter is to address this *why* question.

Men are more likely than women to be victims of all types of
crime except sexual assault (otherwise known as rape). Despite
the gender differences in the prevalence of various forms of crime,
women are more afraid of all types of crime (Karmen 1991).
Why? We would certainly expect them to manifest higher fear of

rape but why do they have higher fear of other crimes? In addition to these questions, we also seek to identify which women are more likely to be afraid of sexual assault and the other victimizations.

THE SHADOW OF SEXUAL ASSAULT

According to recent crime data, women's rate for victimization due to violent crime—excluding rape—is about three-fifths of the rate for men. When one considers changes over time, however, "the difference between men's and women's rates of victimization from violent crime has slowly decreased" (Harlow 1991, p. 1). This is in part due to the increase in the rate of rape (sexual assault) which has more than quadrupled since 1960 (see Figure 4–1 for details). Although some men report being sexually assaulted, the rate of sexual assault for women has consistently been over ten times that of the rate for men (Harlow 1991). But increases in other violent crimes, especially those committed by intimates, probably also contribute to higher fear (Dean and deBruyn-Kops 1982; Harlow 1991). Nevertheless, the finding that women are more afraid of crime is one that has been established in the literature for years—even before the crime wave of the late 1960s and early 1970s.

Most scholarly discussion of women's higher levels of fear generally hinges on the horror of rape, whether from strangers or acquaintances, that may attend any other crime (Gordon and Riger 1989; Hindelang et al. 1978; Riger et al. 1978; Smith 1988). Theories of why rape occurs are numerous but most recent ones focus on gender inequality, pornography, social disorganization, and the cultural acceptance of legitimate violence (Baron and Straus 1989; Bourque 1989; Sacco 1990). Rape is a particularly vexing experience and women are especially susceptible to it. The physical pain and harm caused by rape is horrible but women's accounts of the emotional and psychological damage indicate that it is often worse; and the intensity of the emotional pain endures for years—albeit sometimes in latent form (Gordon and Riger 1989; Parks 1990; Schram 1978; Wirtz and Harrell 1987).

Consider the following information from the "police blotter" in a newspaper serving a university community.

> 8:30 a.m. Police received a report of a window peeker at the southeast corner of Earhart Residence Hall. The suspect is a

white male with a black mustache and collar-length wavy hair. He is in his late 20s to early 30s and is approximately 5 feet 11 inches tall. The suspect was seen wearing a navy blue jacket. Case is under investigation.

While all people might be concerned about window peekers, the fact that the offender is a "peeping Tom" at a women's dormitory makes the case especially disturbing to women. Perhaps the assailant was intent on burlary and was just waiting for vacant rooms. Yet, a male window peeker at a female dormitory raises the specter of sexual assault coupled with any other type of offense.

In a sense, then, *any* victimization of women may involve the possibility of sexual assault. In discussing fear of victimization, Warr (1984) asserts that there are *perceptually contemporaneous offenses*—offenses which people may associate with any victimization (e.g., burglary of one's home while the occupant is present could lead to assault or murder). Rape certainly qualifies as a perceptually contemporaneous offense to most crimes; but its uniqueness as a form of victimization to women probably escalates the degree of fear attending other crimes committed against women. In other words, sexual assault may "shadow" other types of victimization among women. Rape may operate like a "master offense" among women, especially younger women who have the highest rate of rape, heightening fear reactions for other forms of crime. If this is the case, one would expect fear of rape to correlate with other forms of fear and to add uniquely to explaining fear of other types of crime.

For the specific aims of this chapter, I advocate considering rape as a special type of perceptually contemporaneous offense. When women consider any type of victimization, one of the first considerations is the possibility of sexual assault coupled with the other offense. Whereas there is no widespread precedent in criminology or victimization studies to dichotomize crime such that one category is sexual assault and the other includes everything else, perhaps some justification for my doing so is in order.[2] I have consistently throughout my work referred to the conventional distinction of personal or violent crime and property crime. And as often found, I too discovered that robbery fits with latent variables for both personal and property crime. Yet, for the purpose of this chapter it may be useful to lay aside the conventional nomenclature in order to consider how men and women interpret victimization possibilities and react accordingly.

Whereas women are uniquely susceptible to rape, it appears that a "shadow of sexual assault" is latent in most any victimization of women. Rather than simply refer to them as "other crimes," I use the term *nonsexual crime* to distinguish it from sexual crime (rape). Of course, some men are raped by women and some men are raped by other men. But the vast majority of rape in the United States occurs where a man (or men) victimize a woman. Another term which may substitute for nonsexual crime is "nongendered crime" emphasizing the sexuality and gender identity of the actors. I prefer using the term nonsexual crime because of its convenient contrast with sexual crime. Perhaps it is pedantic but I want it to be clear that my use of the term sexual crime refers to the *behavior* of the offense not the *motivation* for it. Victimization scholars have long shown that rape is not simply an act motivated by *sexual* desire and aggression but rape motivation clearly draws upon tendencies toward violence and domination (Bourque 1989; Gordon and Riger 1989). I recognize the exploratory nature of the typology of sexual and nonsexual crime but introduce it in an attempt to help us better understand why women have higher fear of all types of crime (even though they have lower rates of victimization for all crimes except rape). As will become evident, there is empirical justification for this dichotomy as well.

Consistent with most previous research, data from the Fear of Crime in America survey also show that women are more fearful of all of the ten offenses considered; the differences are greater for the violent personal crimes including rape, burglary, and robbery. But the difference in fear of sexual assault is dramatic. Women in our sample were more afraid of rape than murder. Figure 7–1 shows the differences between men and women for perceived risk and fear of rape. Figure 7–2 presents parallel information for nonsexual crime.[3] (Table C–5 of the Appendix presents means and standard deviations of fear and perceived risk by sex for each type of crime.) Similar to findings presented by Warr (1984), these data show that fear is consistently higher for women but this is not necessarily the case when making comparisons of perceived risk.

Note from Figure 7–1 that women do not estimate their risk of rape to be very high; women judge their risk of burglary while away from their home, approach by a beggar, and auto theft as

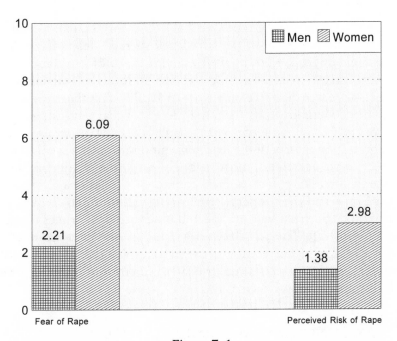

Figure 7–1
Sex Differences in Fear and Perceived Risk of Rape

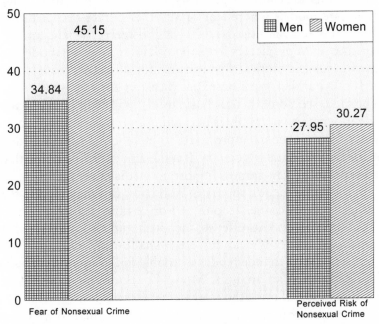

Figure 7–2
Sex Differences in Fear and Perceived Risk of Nonsexual Crime

higher than their risk of rape (see Table C–5 for details). Despite
the generally low level of perceived risk of rape, fear of rape is
quite high. Indeed, rape as well as both types of burglary and
physical attack (assault) manifest very high levels of fear among
women—greater than five on a scale of 10. The fact that rape and
the violent victimizations have high levels of fear suggests some
support to the "shadow of sexual assault" thesis. Also, examining
the correlation matrix of the fear items among women reveals that
fear of rape correlates most strongly with the victimizations
explicitly involving face-to-face contact. Correlations between
fear of rape and the property crimes range from .27 to .53 while
correlations between fear of rape and other personal crimes range
from .64 to .79. The parallel correlations among men are much
smaller. Also, the correlation between perceived risk of rape and
fear of rape is quite substantial (r = .50): even modest levels of perceived rape risk are sufficient to spark intense fear of rape.

FEAR OF NONSEXUAL CRIME: ARE SHADOWS REAL?

To probe this idea more rigorously, the next step is to estimate
multivariate models where fear of all other crimes except rape—
referred to here as nonsexual fear—is considered dependent. The
same basic set of predictors from the risk interpretation model will
be used in a basic model (the measures for official crime and perceived risk parallel the nonsexual measure for fear—all crimes
except rape; see note 3). This basic model will then be compared
to one in which two variables pertaining to rape are added to the
analysis. First, it seems appropriate to include the official rate of
rape for the respondent's county. Rape is a high profile crime that,
when reported, often garners important media coverage. If rape is
high in the respondent's county of residence, this may elevate fear
for other types of crime. Second, if fear of rape is truly a perceptually contemporaneous offense, then it should also influence fear
of nonsexual crime. We can test this "shadowing" effect by adding fear of rape as an independent variable to the equation.[4] Table
7–1 presents such an analysis. Model I excludes the rape covariates while model II adds the relevant rape variables.

The results from the first column are fairly similar to what was
observed earlier in tests of the risk interpretation model (detailed
in chapter 5). We see the same types of effects due to age (the

reverse j-shaped curve), gender, education, perceived risk, and constrained behavior as were observed in earlier models using all victimizations. When rape is excluded from the indicators of official crime, perceived risk, and fear, however, it should be noted that official crime risk ceases to make a significant contribution to the prediction equation for nonsexual crime fear. Recall from chapter 5 that the effect of official crime risk in the models of all crimes was not substantial but it was, in fact, significant for overall crime as well as for personal crime fear. According to model I, actual prevalence of nonsexual crime does not shape fear of nonsexual crime.

Model II, where we add the covariates for rape, reveals some intriguing findings. To begin, note the fairly substantial increase in explained variance, to a total of 64 percent (this is more than a 50 percent increase in explained variance). This increment to R^2 is principally due to the addition of fear of rape. The official rape rate is also significant but barely so. (Despite the weak effects, it is true that the official rape rate is more important than the official rate of nonsexual crime in predicting fear of nonsexual crime.)

The magnitude of the effect due to fear is striking. Indeed, the effects due to fear of rape and perceived risk of nonsexual crime are about equal—added evidence of the shadow thesis. What is even more intriguing is that the coefficient for gender is *nonsignificant* in model II. That is, once one controls for fear of rape, women are not more afraid of other types of crime, perhaps even strengthening the use of the nomenclature of nonsexual crime. Women are more afraid of nonsexual crime but it is principally due to their perceived risk of such crime and their fear of rape.

Most of the other effects noted in model I persist but a few effects are different in size. First, the age effect is not as strong. There is still a curvilinear relationship between age and fear but instead of it resembling a reverse j-shape, it is much flatter (more of an uneven u-shape). Second, the effect of constrained behavior is still significant but less substantial. Regardless of what people have done to avoid crime or defend themselves against criminal activity, such actions are still associated with somewhat higher levels of fear.

Models I and II were also estimated for the subsample of women (reported in the Appendix, Table C–6). The results of model I are very similar to those presented for the full sample except that official risk of nonsexual crime is significant in pre-

Table 7–1
Predicting Fear of Nonsexual Crime

Independent Variables	Model I	Model II
ECOLOGICAL		
Official Crime (nonsexual)	-.00[a]	-.00
	-.05[b]	-.09
South[c]	-1.62	-1.29
	-.04	-.03
West	-1.88	-1.48
	-.04	-.03
North East	.76	.19
	.02	.01
Urban	1.94	1.60
	.04	.03
NEIGHBORHOOD		
Incivility	-.52	-.14
	-.03	-.01
Crime Watch	-.13	.07
	-.00	.00
PERSONAL		
Age	-.52**	-.29*
	-.44	-.24
Age^2	.00*	.00*
	.41	.28
Gender (women)	6.80**	-1.67
	.17	-.04
Race (nonwhite)	2.14	1.47
	.04	.03
Education	-1.17**	-.96**
	-.07	-.06
Health	-.29	-.52
	-.01	-.02

Independent Variables	Model I	Model II
Housing Tenure	.19	-.02
	.01	-.00
Victimization	-.57	-1.67
	-.01	-.03
Indirect Victimization	2.00	.52
	.05	.01
Perceived Risk (nonsexual)	.66**	.71**
	.50	.54
Constrained Behavior	4.12**	2.56**
	.15	.10
RAPE		
Official Rape Rate		.00*
		.09
Fear of Rape		3.41**
		.54
Intercept	32.31	29.25
R^2	.40	.64

[a]Unstandardized coefficient.
[b]Standardized coefficient.
[c]Midwest serves as the reference group for the regional comparisons.
*p ≤ .05.
**p ≤ .01.

dicting fear. The results of model II on the subsample of women are generally similar to those for the full sample but there are notable exceptions. First, the effects for education and constrained behavior are nonsignificant among the female subsample. The other difference is that the effect of fear of rape is slightly greater than the effect due to perceived risk of nonsexual crime (beta values of .62 and .58 respectively). Among women, fear of rape is the most important determinant of fear of nonsexual crime. In other words, women are more afraid of crime but it is largely because they are afraid of rape.

FEAR OF RAPE?

If fear of rape is the major determinant of fear of nonsexual crime among women, then the next logical question is what heightens fear of rape? The results of a regression analysis to identify the factors that influence fear of rape are presented in Table 7–2. The first column presents results for all women while the latter two are specific to age groups. In the first column, the official rape rate is negatively associated with fear of rape, and fear of rape is generally higher in the northeastern region of the country. The age relationship is significant but no curvilinear relationship is evident: younger women are most afraid of rape. The most important determinant of fear of rape is perceived risk of rape. Constrained behavior also affects fear of rape in the manner consistent with earlier findings—constraining one's behavior actually heightens fear.

Seeing the impact of age in shaping rape, the sample was next divided into age groups to examine the effects more closely. Again, it is the youngest women who are most afraid of rape. By breaking age into the seven categories used in the previous chapter and conducting a multiple classification analysis, the youngest age group (18–24) expressed the highest fear, 7.37, while women in the 65–74 age range expressed the least fear, 5.26. With a grand mean of 6.1 on a scale of one to ten, it is quite clear that fear of rape is high, especially among the youngest women.[5] What is intriguing is that this age group of women is precisely the category which is most likely to be victimized by some type of sexual assault. Estimates vary but women age 18–24 probably have a rape rate over 4 per 1,000 based on victimization data—not based on official statistics of reported rape (Harlow 1991). The rate for women 25–34 is approximately 2.3 per 1,000 women while the rate falls to below 1 per 1,000 after age 35 (the rates differ by ethnicity, with African Americans having higher victimization rates at all ages). Thus, the high levels of fear among young women are not surprising given victimization rates.

Given the absence of a significant curvilinear relationship by age and the high rate of rape victimization among women 34 years of age and younger, two additional equations are presented in Table 7–2 estimating fear of rape among the two age groups. Note that the explained variance in the younger age group is nearly twice the amount for the older group of women. Among those 18–34 years of age, perceived risk is the single most important predictor of fear of rape followed by constrained behavior, housing tenure, and age. Even among women age 18–34, the age relationship is strong, demonstrating the keen fear among the youngest women. The effect of housing tenure is negative, indicating that women who have more recently moved are more afraid of rape. The overall picture of the fear experienced by these women is vexing to say the least. They feel their risk of rape is high and they have recently taken measures to reduce their risk of being victimized due to any crime; yet, the youngest ones, who are quite likely to relocate due to career and family transitions, experience dread in daily life and especially just after moving to new housing. It is a haunting spector of existence in a society in which violence and sexual subjugation is rampant.

For women 35 years of age and older, their fear is generally lower and almost totally shaped by perceived risk. Fear is higher among the younger women in this analysis, again reflecting congruence with victimization rate data. Note also that women in the northeastern portion of the country have greater fear of rape; no regional effects were observed among the younger women but regional differences among the more mature women are about equal to the age effect.

"TAKE BACK THE . . . DAY"

Women took to American streets in the late 1970s to launch a "Take back the night" campaign. Women's groups recognized, as did Marshall Fishwick, that "the tendency to identify manhood with a capacity for physical violence has a long history in America." Rape is an atrocious act of physical violence that plagues more and more women each year. Protests and pleas have continued over the years to make our streets safer, but rape continues to haunt the lives of millions of American women. It is not just a fear of being on the streets at night that concerns and haunts so many women. It is a fear that pervades much of the daily life of women, especially younger women, whether they are getting into their cars

Table 7-2
Predicting Fear of Rape Among Women

Independent Variables	All Women (N = 554)	Age 18–34 (N = 173)	Age 35+ (N = 381)
ECOLOGICAL			
Official Crime (rape)	-.00[a]*	-.00	-.00
	-.11[b]	-.13	-.09
South[c]	-.17	-.33	-.08
	-.02	-.05	-.01
West	.10	.07	.11
	.01	.01	.01
North East	.83*	.93	.10*
	.10	.12	.12
Urban	.41	.65	.25
	.04	.07	.03
NEIGHBORHOOD			
Incivility	-.14	-.17	-.14
	-.05	-.07	-.05
Crime Watch	.28	-.33	.42
	.03	-.03	.04
PERSONAL			
Age	-.09*	-.12**	-.03*
	-.45	-.19	-.13
Age^2	.00	—	—
	.30		
Race (nonwhite)	.26	.24	.15
	.03	.03	.01
Education	-.21	-.22	-.18
	-.06	-.07	-.06
Health	.12	.07	.07
	.02	.01	.02

Independent Variables	All Women (N = 554)	Age 18–34 (N = 173)	Age 35+ (N = 381)
Housing Tenure	-.05	-.64**	.12
	-.02	-.24	.06
Victimization	.26	.41	.25
	.03	.05	.03
Indirect Victimization	.33	-.13	.65
	.05	-.02	.08
Perceived Risk (rape)	.43**	.43**	.45**
	.29	.32	.30
Constrained Behavior	.66**	1.17**	.42
	.13	.25	.08
Intercept	6.68	10.54	4.60
R^2	.21	.30	.16

[a]Unstandardized coefficient.
[b]Standardized coefficient.
[c]Midwest serves as the reference group for the regional comparisons.
*$p \leq .05$.
**$p \leq .01$.

after a day of work or out on a shopping trip. Surely, the fear is most serious at night but women appear conscious of how they must adjust their lives at all times of the day. Might any actions or interactions escalate to sexual assault? This is the question that women face all too often. Indeed, one gauge of their freedom is whether or not this question drifts from consciousness (i.e., Can women "stop thinking" about sexual assault?).

The results of this investigation show that fear of rape is very high among younger women reflecting national victimization data. Younger women who often move during educational, career, or family transitions are especially afraid of crime when they are in new environments. Despite their attempts to avoid victimization, fear of rape influences their daily life. Women in the northeastern regions of the United States are also more likely to be afraid of rape but this is because of the higher than expected levels of fear among women in this region who are 35 years of age or older. It matters not whether women have been personally victimized; the imaginative horror of sexual assault is sufficient to spark such fear.

Gordon and Riger (1989) studied rape and fear of rape in three American cities—Chicago, Philadelphia, and San Francisco—and document both the pervasiveness and the dread of what they call the "female fear." They found that "some women say they would *rather* die than be raped and live. For many women, to be raped is, in essence, to die. Some women have killed themselves after surviving rape attacks, and many other victims consider it" (p. 9). Gordon and Riger (1989) go on to argue that rape is the most stigmatizing form of victimization, imploding on every domain of life and personhood (see also Riger and Gordon 1981).

Not only are women afraid of rape itself but the present investigation shows clearly that fear of rape influences fear of other types of crime. Although robbery, assault, and murder are examples of nonsexual crime, women's fear of them is strongly shaped by their fear of sexual crime: one's ability to predict fear of nonsexual crime is substantially improved if we also consider fear of sexual crime. Indeed, when one does so, the gender effect disappears. Women are more afraid of all types of crime but this fear is largely due to fear of sexual assault. I depict this phenomenon as the analogy of the "shadow of sexual assault."

Rape can be seen as another outcome of any victimization, but it is especially germane to those offenses which involve face-to-face contact—a perceptually contemporaneous offense as described by Warr (1984). Resisting a robber or struggling against an assault can be effective; yet, the possibility exists that it will not, and that resistance itself could inflame some offenders. Regardless of whether or not one resists or attempts to fight off an offender, sexual assault of women is a contingency for any face-to-face offense, especially when the offense is committed by a man or a group of men.[6] It appears that when women think about the possibility of victimization, they also contemplate the likelihood of sexual assault for a given offense.

Supplementary analyses where each of the nonsexual crimes was treated as dependent showed that the effect of rape fear on each offense varies across the type of crime considered. For example, the effect of fear of rape on fear of murder is quite strong (beta = .62). On the other hand, the effect of fear of rape on fear of car theft is quite modest although also significant (beta = .18). These and other findings give substantial support to the shadow thesis: fear of rape shadows other victimization fears and the degree of the effect is associated with personal contact and seriousness of the offense. The list of victimizations used here examines offenses where there is a fairly high probability of personal contact. It would be useful in future research to add other victimizations which would not involve face-to-face contact (e.g., mail-order fraud). If the shadow thesis is correct, the effect of fear of rape on such crime should be less strong or even nonexistent.

Given the findings presented here, it seems appropriate to recommend that women's fear of crime merits detailed attention on both the policy and research fronts. If one wants to reduce fear of crime among women, confronting the prevalence of sexual assault against women should receive high priority. Obviously, some effort should be expended toward defensive maneuvers in the face of such assault but the bulk of the effort should be toward the *prevention* of sexual assault.

In a thoughtful and thorough study of why rape occurs in the United States, Baron and Straus (1989) identify four major reasons. They found that the single most important predictor of the prevalence of rape in the fifty states is the circulation rate for sexual or pornographic magazines. Other factors in descending order of importance include social disorganization, gender inequality, and the cultural acceptance of legitimate violence. These four factors are clearly related. States with high rates of pornographic magazine circulation are states which also manifest considerable social disorganization, gender inequality, and legitimated violence. As such there appears to be an ecological structure to the subjugation of women. Heterosexual pornography, especially the "hard core" variety, reflects and promotes the male domination of women as it sexually objectifies women. Moreover, there is increasing evidence that physical acts of violence against women in pornographic materials serve as behavior models of assault (U.S. Attorney General's Commission on Pornography 1986). Taken together, these findings suggest that a sober analysis of the culture of male dominance is needed as manifested in gender inequality on the economic and social front and in the legitimation of violence (Longino 1980).

As pertains to date rape, one can see how the culture of male dominance affects perceptions of what sexual behaviors are tolerable when dating. In short, the male cultural model is often somewhat permissive of rape as men feel that "a little force" is to be expected in many sexual encounters (Kanin 1985). A man may claim—as is often done in court—that a woman has "led him on." Perhaps convictions for some of these cases, especially the highly visible ones (e.g., Mike Tyson), will clarify the popular definition of rape so as to include *any* use of force or coercion for sexual activity at any time in the social encounter.

To conclude this chapter, let us return to a statment by Baumer (1978) which I mentioned at the beginning of this chapter: "we know who is afraid but very little about why they are afraid" (p. 254). Despite women's generally lower level of victimization in all offenses except rape, we have long known that women are more afraid of all types of crime. Why they fear rape does not need reiteration. Using these data, why women fear nonsexual crime appears to be largely due to the possibility of sexual crime contingent with any blatantly nonsexual crime. If one uses fear of rape as a predictor of nonsexual crime, the explained variance jumps about 50 percent and the gender effect disappears. Women, especially younger women who are most often the targets of rape, are more afraid of nonsexual crime but it is largely due to their fear of sexual crime. Women are aware of the atrocity of rape in American society; the younger women see the shadow both day and night.

CHAPTER 8

Constraints on Daily Living

I must create a system or be enslaved by another man's.

William Blake

The greater Miami, Florida area needed to do something to turn things around. Normally, Miami is a hot spot for vacationers, but tourists cooled to the prospect of spending time there in 1993. Of course, any big city has its share of crime, but Miami was quickly earning a reputation for a city replete with senseless or "random crime." People did not need to be in on a drug deal to fall victim to crime—they could just be vacationing.

A German woman was simply on a tourist trek when two teenagers robbed her. Perhaps as an afterthought, they then ran her over with a car. They had her goods, but they wanted to do more—almost for sport.

After this and several other horrible acts of violent crime were reported in a relatively short period, tourism to the southeast coast of Florida dropped appreciably. Tourists had judged the area to have too much risk. This situation serves to highlight another feature of the risk interpretation model, that of behavioral adaptations to high perceived risk.

When an actor perceives risk to be high, jeopardizing something of value, a variety of reactions may ensue. Using the risk interpretation model, there are two domains of such reactions which have been considered as people face crime risk: affectual and behavioral. While we have considered both these domains throughout, the emphasis of earlier chapters was on the affectual domain—and fear in particular. The purpose of this chapter is to give more detailed consideration to people's different behavioral responses. In other words, the focus is on what people *do* to cope with crime. Some may avoid Miami as a vacation destination. Some may turn to defensive behaviors such as keeping a weapon in their home or carrying a gun or mace. Others may turn to avoidance behaviors such as staying out of areas during the day or night. And most will combine defensive and avoidance behaviors into an overall lifestyle for coping with crime. Who are the people likely to engage in such activities? Are such behaviors ecologically patterned or are they primarily based on personal characteristics? These are the questions pursued here.

GUNS AND DOGS: FRONTIER TOOLS FOR NEIGHBORHOODS AND SUBWAYS?

While there have been dozens of studies of the antecedents of fear of crime, there have been comparatively few studies of how people attempt to cope with crime.[1] A considerable portion of the existing research has been offered in an attempt to identify whether fear of crime increases the likelihood of either taking defensive actions or spurring avoidance behaviors. Defensive and avoidance behaviors are the two main areas of *risk-reduction* activity but the research has often been framed as a response to fear of crime. The fact that previous research frames the analysis as a reaction to fear should not surprise us if we also consider that many of the same studies do not explicitly include a discussion of the concept of risk or perceived risk of crime.

Although there are differences in what is reported in previous research, it appears that the effects of fear of crime on most types of constrained behavior are either trivial or nonexistent (DuBow et al. 1979; Wright 1991). Among the studies reporting positive effects of fear on constrained behavior, most of them do not explicitly consider the concept of risk in their models (e.g., Liska et al. 1988; Taylor et al. 1986). When studies include risk or perceived risk in the analysis, the findings generally show that fear of crime is inconsequential or that its effects are trivial and indirect (e.g., Bankston and Thompson 1989; Hindelang et al. 1978). Based on previous research and the risk interpretation model, therefore, I place constrained behavior as a response to perceived risk in a causal sequence of events. To reiterate, fear and constrained behavior are two responses to high perceived risk of victimization. It is conceivable that fear can also influence constrained behavior, but a test for such a possibility in chapter five found no evidence for that hypothesis. Rather, constrained behavior and fear were both likely outcomes of high perceived risk, and constraining behavior actually heightened fear.

What is quite clear from the research literature is that women and older people are generally more likely to take precautionary measures, especially by avoiding potentially dangerous urban areas both day and night (Kleinman and David 1973; Liska et al. 1988; Skogan and Maxfield 1981). Hindelang et al. (1978) also found that such avoidance or precautionary measures were not drastic changes in lifestyle but fairly subtle modifications in daily routines: "rather than making substantial changes in *what* they do, people tend to change the *ways* in which they do things" (p. 224). For instance, such subtle modifications may include changes in traffic routes, asking for an accompaniment from a friend or acquaintance, or making "home improvements." It is also clear that sales of security devices and systems continue to grow but little is known about who purchases such systems except that homeowners and more affluent residents are generally more likely to acquire such products.

While women are more likely to engage in avoidance behaviors, they are also more likely to carry mace or other nonlethal defensive devices. When it comes to firearms, however, men are much more likely to both own and carry guns. Indeed, a sizable proportion of the previous research on coping with crime has examined firearm ownership and carrying guns, especially handguns. Wright (1991) summarizes the available evidence on ownership: "Despite the apparently widespread impression to the contrary, owning a firearm primarily for self-defense is itself relatively uncommon" (p. 452). He finds that about three-fourths of the firearms are owned for reasons other than self-defense, such as sport, recreation, defense against animals, or keeping a family heirloom. Even among *handgun* owners, sport and recreation are mentioned about as often as self-defense. The literature is quite consistent in showing that men and rural residents are more likely to be owners (DeFronzo 1979).

Bankston and Thompson (1989; see also Bankston et al. 1990) claim that carrying a firearm is a much more precise and relevant measure than gun ownership when studying the "use" of firearms for protection. Their research shows two factors to be most important in predicting carrying a firearm. Based on a survey of Louisiana drivers, they found that "southern culture" and the belief that weapons deter victimization (which appears to be part of the southern culture) account for most of the explained variance in predicting who carries a firearm. They do not conclude that the south is given to a culture of violence but simply a culture of guns—guns are commonplace and believed to be useful. Again, both their research and that on gun ownership show strong differences by gender—men are much more likely to own and carry firearms.

As mentioned earlier, our measure of constrained behavior includes a wide set of adaptive behaviors. Beyond avoidance and firearm protection, other types of defensive actions were probed. Figure 8–1 portrays the distribution of each of the ten responses. The actions considered were explicitly identified as something "people do to reduce their risk to crime." Although we cannot be sure that crime prevention was the sole motivation for such actions, we framed the questions so that crime prevention was salient in the mind of the respondent (i.e., risk reduction was at least partly responsible for undertaking the action). The ten items were used in earlier chapters as a latent variable termed constrained behavior but are treated separately here to better understand the specific actions undertaken by the respondents.

The most common form of behavioral adaptation to crime is avoiding unsafe areas at night. Given that over three-fourths of the respondents report avoiding unsafe areas at night, this is one more bit of evidence about the conspicuous artificiality of the purported "fear of crime" measures available in the NCS and GSS. Those surveys ask respondents to rate their safety and fear of being out alone at night in their neighborhood (or within one mile) while the vast majority of respondents in this survey say that they purposefully avoid unsafe areas at night. In other words, the "fear" measures garnered in both the NCS and GSS tap situations that most people routinely avoid. How realistic are they, then, for measuring how people feel about crime in *their* lives?

Figure 8–1 shows that beyond avoiding unsafe areas at night, other actions undertaken by a majority of the sample studied here include adding locks to one's home, adding outside lighting, and avoiding unsafe areas during the day. While over 42 percent of American households have at least one dog, only about 25 percent of our respondents report buying a dog, at least in part, for its role as a watchdog (American Veterinary Medical Association 1983). Less than one in five respondents report carrying some type of a defensive object such as a gun or mace but over 40 percent report

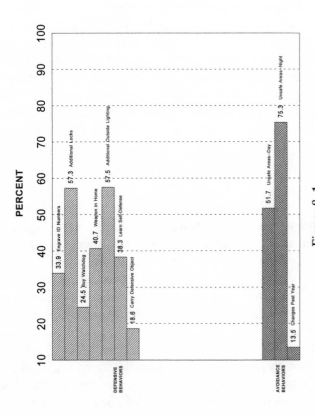

Figure 8–1

Percent of Respondents Constraining Behavior

having a weapon in their home. Finally, only 13.5 percent report changing their daily activities in the past year because of crime.

Consistent with what Hindelang et al. (1978) report, people tend to approach crime coping mechanisms with fairly stable "lifestyle" approaches. Some changes are being made each year to help respondents deal with the threat of different victimizations ranging from car-jacking to burglary, but most adults settle into a *lifestyle* that they perceive as adequate to the potential risk they face. When we couple the individual items into the construct of constrained behavior, it is quite clear that most Americans engage in more than one or two such actions. Indeed, a simple sum of these ten items yields a mean score of 4.1 with a median of 4. It is clear that there is a repertoire of actions and devices—dogs, guns, and lights included—upon which Americans draw to reduce their risk of criminal victimization. Most actions are targeted toward avoiding victimization in unsafe areas and protecting one's home.

PATTERNS OF PROTECTION

Constrained behavior, treated as a latent variable, was earlier found to be higher among respondents with high levels of perceived risk of crime as well as among women (see chapter 5). It was also higher among residents of the south, among people in their 50s and 60s, and in urban areas and counties with high official crime rates. The risk interpretation model explains over half of the variance in constrained behavior; and higher constrained behavior is associated with higher levels of fear (similar but not identical to the findings reported by Liska et al. 1988). In an attempt to identify who is most likely to undertake each of the behaviors considered, it may be useful to continue with the decomposition of the construct of constrained behavior but now in multivariate analyses.

Table 8–1 presents logistic regression estimates for each of the defensive measures probed among the respondents.[2] Beginning with the first column, the prediction of engraving identification numbers on valuables, this practice is less common in the northeastern part of the country and among those affiliated with a crime watch program. The addition of locks to doors and windows is more likely in the south but less likely among those affiliated with a crime watch program. Apparently belonging to a crime watch program provides some degree of perceived safety to respondents, thereby softening initiatives toward at least some of the defensive actions. White persons, those who lived in their housing unit longer, and those with higher perceived risk are also more likely to add locks to their homes. There is a curvilinear relationship between age and the purchase of a watchdog: the likelihood increases through the adult years and then decreases somewhat in later life. Owning a watchdog is also more common among persons with lower educational attainment as well as among those who have lived in their home longer or been victimized during the past year.[3]

Turning to keeping a weapon in one's home for protection, this is the only instance in which official crime risk influences the action. Note, however, that the effect is modest and negative. People in counties with lower crime rates are more likely to keep a weapon in their home. Consistent with earlier research, keeping a gun or other weapon in the home is also much more likely in the south and among male respondents. This behavior is less likely among residents of the northeast, those with higher educational attainment, and those who have lived in their home for a short period.[4]

Adding outside lights to one's home is more likely in the northeast but less likely in urban areas. It is more common among women, those living in their homes for longer periods of time, and those who sense risk to be high. Learning about self-defense is less common among respondents who participate in crime watch programs and older people. Indirect victimization and perceived risk of victimization both increase the likelihood of learning more about self-defense. Finally, carrying an object for self-defense is less common in the western states but more common among women and those who live in neighborhoods characterized by high levels of incivility. Carrying a defensive object is also more likely among those who see their risk of crime to be high.

Reflecting on these findings, it is interesting to see how different predictors affect the various outcomes. It is somewhat surprising that perceived risk affects only four out of the seven options considered. Nonetheless, perceived risk and housing tenure are the most consistent predictors of the defensive measures. Housing tenure probably reflects home ownership as well as familiarity with and attachments to the neighborhood. This is especially the case in those instances where the defensive measures are also

Table 8-1

Predicting Defensive Behaviors: Logistic Regression Estimates

Independent Variables	ID Numbers	Added Locks	Watchdog	Weapon/ Home	Outside Lights	Learn Defense	Carried Object
ECOLOGICAL							
Official Crime	-1.5e-6[a]	1.0e-6	-2.1e-6	-2.5e-6*	-1.7e-6	-2.4e-7	-1.2e-6
	1.1e-6[b]	1.1e-6	1.3e-6	1.1e-6	1.0e-6	1.0e-6	1.3e-6
South[c]	-.07	.33*	.06	.81**	.32	.07	.16
	.18	.17	.20	.18	.17	.17	.21
West	.10	.34	.13	.33	.19	-.13	-.86**
	.21	.20	.23	.21	.20	.21	.30
Northeast	-.55**	.15	-.15	-.44*	.41*	-.25	-.14
	.20	.19	.22	.20	.19	.20	.24
Urban	-.33	.32	-.33	-.26	-.41*	-.28	-.04
	.19	.18	.20	.19	.19	.19	.24
NEIGHBORHOOD							
Incivility	.10	.06	.03	.10	-.02	.00	.20**
	.06	.06	.07	.06	.06	.06	.07

Independent Variables	ID Numbers	Added Locks	Watchdog	Weapon/Home	Outside Lights	Learn Defense	Carried Object
Crime Watch	-.92**	-.56*	-.23	-.24	-.25	-.53**	-.45
	.20	.22	.23	.21	.21	.20	.24
PERSONAL							
Age	.04	.02	.07*	.01	.01	-.05*	.01
	.02	.02	.03	.02	.02	.02	.03
Age^2	-3.9e-4	-2.0e-4	-1.1e-3**	-3.0e-4	-1.2e-4	3.8e-4	-2.6e-4
	2.4e-4	2.3e-4	3.0e-4	2.5e-4	2.3e-4	2.4e-4	3.2e-4
Gender (women)	-.09	.25	.29	-.60**	.44**	.12	.39*
	.14	.13	.15	.14	.13	.14	.18
Race (nonwhite)	-.33	-.50**	-.40	-.19	-.06	.34	-.03
	.21	.19	.24	.20	.19	.19	.24
Education	.08	.05	-.14*	-.35**	.08	-.02	-.08
	.06	.06	.07	.07	.06	.06	.08
Health	.03	.03	.10	.03	.08	.05	-.03
	.10	.09	.11	.10	.09	.10	.12
Housing Tenure	.08	.12*	.26**	.15**	.19**	.01	.09
	.05	.05	.06	.06	.05	.05	.07

Table 8–1 (continued)

Independent Variables	ID Numbers	Added Locks	Watchdog	Weapon/ Home	Outside Lights	Learn Defense	Carried Object
Victimization	.21	.20	.44*	.33	.11	-.06	.07
	.18	.18	.19	.18	.18	.18	.21
Indirect Victimization	-.10	.13	.21	.15	.19	.32*	-.05
	.15	.15	.17	.15	.15	.15	.19
Perceived Risk	.01	.02**	.00	.01	.01*	.02**	.02**
	.00	.01	.01	.00	.00	.00	.01
Intercept	.03	-.83	-2.40	.08	-.83	1.41	-1.18
	.80	.80	.92	.81	.78	.79	.99
Chi Squared[d]	55.86**	75.46**	68.04**	132.67**	56.93**	66.65**	65.56**
Explained Variance	.05	.07	.06	.11	.05	.06	.06

[a]Unstandardized coefficient. Scientific notation used for parameter estimates of official crime and age squared.
[b]Standard error.
[c]Midwest serves as the reference group for the regional comparisons.
[d]Each equation has 17 degrees of freedom.

* $p \leq .05$.
** $p \leq .01$.

"home improvements"—adding locks and outside lights.[5] It is also interesting to note how important region of the country is in predicting the various adaptive mechanisms. Southerners are more likely to add locks and to have weapons in the home while northeastern residents add outside lights. It appears there really is a culture of coping with crime which varies by ecological context.

Crime watch programs apparently provide some degree of perceived safety pre-empting the activation of three types of constrained behavior: adding identification numbers, adding locks, and learning self-defense. Age differences in these behaviors are trivial or nonexistent. In only a few instances were gender differences observed: women have outside lighting added to their homes and are more likely to carry mace or other non-lethal defensive objects while men are more likely to keep firearms available at home. Recalling that the independent variables explained over half of the variance in the latent variable of constrained behavior, it is intriguing to note that the explained variance in these equations is quite modest, ranging from .05 to .11.

Table 8–2 presents parallel equations for the three types of avoidance behaviors. Avoiding unsafe areas during the day is much more likely among urban residents, women, and those with high perceived risk. The age relationship with such behavior is curvilinear—increasing through adulthood but showing a slight decrease in later life. People who were victimized in the past year are less likely to say that they avoid unsafe areas during the day. It is unclear if they were victimized because they do not constrain their actions or if their previous victimization was a nighttime experience, thereby signalling no need to constrain daytime activities.

Turning to avoiding unsafe areas at night, again there is a moderately strong effect from urban areas: urban residents "learn" to survive in the city by avoiding certain areas. Women and those who have shorter housing tenures are more likely to avoid unsafe areas at night. The same is true for people who know of a close friend or relative being victimized in the past year as well as those who perceive their risk to be high.

In the final column, it can be seen that people living in neighborhoods characterized by incivility are more likely to have changed their daily activities during the past year. Women, non-whites, those who experienced direct or indirect victimization,

Table 8–2
Predicting Avoidance Behaviors: Logistic Regression Estimates

Independent Variables	Unsafe Areas: Day	Unsafe Areas: Night	Changes Past Year
ECOLOGICAL			
Official Crime	-1.6e-6[a]	-1.9e-6	-1.7e-6
	1.1e-6[b]	1.5e-6	1.3e-6
South[c]	.26	.39	.32
	.18	.21	.28
West	-.07	.15	.19
	.21	.25	.32
Northeast	-.13	.41	.14
	.20	.23	.32
Urban	.58**	.89**	.13
	.20	.21	.34
NEIGHBORHOOD			
Incivility	-.02	.13	.24**
	.06	.09	.08
Crime Watch	-.12	-.14	.27
	.21	.26	.32
PERSONAL			
Age	.06*	.03	.01
	.02	.03	.04
Age^2	-5.0e-4*	-3.6e-4	-5.0e-6
	2.4e-4	2.8e-4	3.9e-4
Gender (women)	.98**	1.37**	.78**
	.14	.17	.22
Race (nonwhite)	.02	-.05	.74**
	.20	.26	.25
Education	-.05	.11	.12
	.06	.08	.10

Independent Variables	Unsafe Areas: Day	Unsafe Areas: Night	Changes Past Year
Health	.03	.08	.08
	.10	.11	.15
Housing Tenure	-.10	-.20**	-.12
	.05	.07	.08
Victimization	-.50**	-.35	.57*
	.19	.23	.23
Indirect Victimization	.14	.39*	.59**
	.15	.20	.21
Perceived Risk	.04**	.04**	.03**
	.01	.01	.01
Intercept	-2.89	-2.00	-5.57
	.82	.97	1.28
Chi Square[d]	158.70**	196.58**	155.30**
Explained Variance	.13	.16	.13

[a]Unstandardized coefficient. Scientific notation used for parameter estimates of official crime and age squared.
[b]Standard error.
[c]Midwest serves as the reference group for the regional comparisons.
[d]Each equation has seventeen degrees of freedom.
*$p \leq .05$.
**$p \leq .01$.

and those with high perceived risk are also more likely to report making changes in the past year (Skogan 1987).

The explained variance in these equations is somewhat higher but still quite modest (.13 to .16). The only significant direct effect among the ecological variables is for the rural/urban comparison. Urban living virtually requires that one learn how to be "street smart." Unlike what was observed for the defensive measures, none of the regional effects are significant. When personal characteristics are considered, the most consistent and substantial effects are for gender and perceived risk. Women consistently constrain their activities, night and day, and report more changes during the past year to deal with the threat of victimization. As discussed in chapter 7, this is in part due to the perceived risk and seriousness of sexual assault. Even more than what was observed for the defensive measures, perceived risk substantially increases the likelihood that people will take steps to avoid victimization.

QUEST FOR SAFETY IN THE LAND OF FREEDOM

Americans have long prized individualism and personal freedom. Although responsibility is part of the equation defining civility, modern American culture often stresses that individuals should be free to pursue personal goals, unless, of course, they are interfering with the freedom of others (Williams 1970). Crime is one such type of "interference," and evidence from this and other surveys show that increasing numbers of citizens in modern societies must expend considerable time, energy, and money to limit the amount of "interference" they encounter (e.g., Skogan and Maxfield 1981). Most respondents in this survey report taking at least four steps to reduce their threat of criminal victimization.

Firearms are widely owned in the United States and gun purchases continue to be strong; indeed, the sale of firearms recently soared after passage of federal legislation restricting gun ownership. Men have long been the major owners and conveyors of firearms while reports of women's gun ownership have fluctuated considerably over the past twenty years (Maguire and Flanagan 1991). There are reports of an increase in the number of women who are turning to stun-guns and other protective devices for self-defense (Associated Press 1993). Of course, sales of mace for self-protection have been strong for years but now there are even fashions for women who want to carry guns. Unfortunately, as long as violence continues in the nation, Americans will continue to display ingenuity and resourcefulness in designing methods of protection.

Findings from this survey indicate that most respondents tend to feel safe during the day and in familiar surroundings. Yet, the majority also report that they constrain their daily activities at night to avoid potential danger zones. Especially among the urban dwellers, the findings indicate that considerable effort is expended on living "street smart" (Thomas 1967). Residents are socialized to avoid certain areas of town especially at night because of the higher risk of criminal victimization. Gang activity and the threat of robbery, car-jacking, or assault—both sexual and nonsexual—enter the minds of urban dwellers during the course of *routine* daily living. Signs in some subway cars and hallways now inform riders not to make eye contact ("look at") other riders. Both media reports and law enforcement campaigns to educate the public about crime and safety bring criminal victimization into the minds of Americans (Podolefsky and DuBow 1981). If one lives in "the city" or works in the city, coping with crime is a basic part of daily living. It becomes habitual to carry mace, avoid certain areas of town, avoid eye contact, or set the alarm system on one's house or car.[6]

Despite all the precautionary measures people take, however, new forms of crime and new arenas of criminal activity emerge, thereby propelling fresh evaluations of the practice habits. It would appear that the continual process of constraining behavior and then evaluating those practices in light of new forms and arenas of criminality would tend toward a sense of social disorganization. As Park (and Burgess 1967) wrote: "Any form of change that brings any *measurable alteration* in the routine of social life tends to break up habits; and in breaking up the habits upon which existing social organization rests, destroys that organization itself" (emphasis added, p. 107). It is in this sense then that constraining behavior may be clearly seen as escalating fear. When one feels a change in routine is necessary, there may also be a growing cynicism about the social order and the predictability of risk.

Results from this research show that when it comes to what respondents do to avoid or defend themselves against criminal victimization, safety for one's self and family are key. Property crime is important but its significance pales when compared to the trauma of violent personal crime. Most respondents prefer to avoid danger rather than try to work their way out of it. Yet, there are a variety of ways to avoid danger. Most Americans try to steer clear of "trouble" but also feel they need to equip themselves and their homes for various contingencies in a world rife with victimization risk.

CHAPTER 9

Science and Civility: Implications from Risk Interpretation

We cannot work without hoping that others will advance further than we have.

Max Weber

The preceding chapters have examined what fear of crime is and sought to identify the forces that shape it. The approach used throughout this work is based on a risk interpretation model that views constrained behavior and fear of crime as two likely reactions when actors judge their victimization risk to be high. This chapter summarizes the findings from the empirical test of the risk interpretation model and helps one contemplate the implications of the findings. There are two types of implications which will be addressed. First, the scientific implications that relate to our current stock of knowledge on the subject and how subsequent research might fruitfully extend this knowledge. In discussing the scientific implications, I will simultaneously assess what we know and suggest how the research could be extended to enhance our scientific understanding. Second, one's sense of social responsibility implores a consideration of what these findings mean to social life. Social scientists are often strong on criticism but weak on constructive recommendations. Without sounding pontifical, I hope to offer some constructive recommendations for both social policy and science.

IMPLICATIONS FOR CIVILITY: THE QUESTION OF MORAL RELIABILITY?

Consider the following two illustrations regarding criminal victimization in modern society.

Dorothy, a woman in her late seventies, living in central Florida, was quite distraught about her home being burglarized—twice.

117

She had noted that things were changing in her neighborhood but tried to take the precautions she deemed appropriate to protect her home from further offenses. Aware of the need for physical exercise to add "life to her years," she would routinely drive to a local park for brisk morning walks. On one morning, she was accompanied by a friend.

They were about to start their morning walk when her friend realized that she had inadvertently carried her purse along. Seeing no need to carry it, Dorothy offered to take her friend's purse back to her car. While doing so, she was approached by a young man who demanded the purse. She screamed and began to flee, at which time she was shot in the back. The purse was stolen and the young man was on his way.

Banks now routinely advise patrons with "cash machine" cards to beware of people in the vicinity when planning to use an automated banking device. In some cities, men stand near the machines and offer to watch out for patrons in return for a sum of money. Given that some people have been victimized just after completing a transaction, some people find the "sentry" worth the cost. Others are concerned the sentry is, indeed, the robber.

The preceding are just two instances in the arena of human life which illustrate why people think about crime daily. Interpreting victimization risk is a part of our lives—a substantial part for many people, especially city dwellers. Even when we feel we have taken the adequate precautions to prevent it, victimization either directly or vicariously forces its way back into our consciousness. Victimization is so prevalent in modern societies, and especially in America, that it led Stokely Carmichael to once remark that "violence is as American as cherry pie." Eliott Currie stated that "In the severity of its crime rates, the United States more closely resembles the most volatile countries of the Third World than other developed Western societies." Despite the high crime rates in America, the actual frequency of victimization is a tiny fraction of the potential. It is the seriousness of crime and the ensuing experiences that make even the possibility of crime an important consideration in daily life.

Fear of crime is a problem in the United States but this research shows that people are fairly realistic in digesting the mountains of information regarding victimization and interpreting their risk. Although some have argued that fear of crime is a more serious problem than crime itself (Clemente and Kleiman 1976), the findings of the present investigation boldly reach the opposite conclusion. Programs and informal social assistance to allay fear of crime may be appropriate in some cases but "blaming the fear-of-crime victim" is clearly not where our efforts as a nation should be directed. Fear of crime is not the real problem; crime is. Fear of crime is a symptom of a society rife with victimization ranging from child abuse to consumer fraud. Crime is rampant, prisons are full, and there appears to be no turning point in sight. These concerns are not new to sociological thinkers; their magnitude is, however, unique.

Several pioneers in sociology were concerned about how all of the social change that modern societies experience would affect the organization of human civility. Ferdinand Toennies (1963 [1887]) welcomed the rationality of modern societies yet was troubled by the growing sense of individualism. He saw modern societies as weakening the sense of community as collective sentiments and moral responsibility were sacrificed for individualism and rationality. Durkheim ([1935] 1895) was somewhat more optimistic than Toennies but saw anomie—a lack of and confusion over norms—as becoming so widespread that society would provide little moral guidance to individuals. Carrying these concerns in American sociology was Robert Park (Park and Burgess 1967, p. 107):

> We are living in such a period of individualization and social disorganization. Everything is in a state of agitation—everything seems to be undergoing change. Society is, apparently, not much more than a congeries and constellation of social atoms.

While some of these assertions may sound overstated, the concerns about normative guidance and basic civility remain.

We are in the midst of major changes in the basic institutions of family, education, communication, and religion, which influence the frequency of criminal activity. There has always been "crime" in each society but agreement about basic elements of civility are now in question in many modern societies—anomie is commonplace.[1] The differentiation of social structures and the complexities of modern life have gradually given way to more complex moral systems, although some may simply describe it as nihilism. In the process, basic elements of social organization have lost their control, their ability to regulate human action. As Lewis and Salem (1986) conclude, "a lack of conformity to conventional values (e.g., 'thou shall not steal')" leads to the disintegration of *moral reliability*. In sociological terms, morality exists but is less predictable; it is based on interest group debate rather than fairly homogeneous moral codes.[2]

As long as this confusion over the normative order exists, crime will probably remain fairly high. And as long as crime is high, victimization will occupy an important part of the interpretive world of citizens and some citizens, especially women, will be afraid. Again, fear of crime is not typically a disorder of the person; it is most often a symptom of a conspicuously incivil world (Wilson 1993).

SCIENTIFIC STUDY:
WHAT WE KNOW AND WHAT WE NEED TO KNOW

Finally, this study leads me to offer some suggestions regarding further research on fear of crime. Building upon my earlier work with Randy LaGrange, the survey data used here document quite clearly that perceived risk of crime and fear of crime are distinct phenomena. Although the two have been treated interchangeably in some previous research, and risk has been virtually ignored in other studies, the findings from this investigation show that there are important differences in how people judge or assess their risk of victimization versus their fear of such eventualities. This study also shows that despite being ignored in many previous studies, fear of crime is largely shaped by one's perceived risk of victimization. Thus, fear of crime does not appear to be an irrational response by people out of touch with reality.[3] Perceived risk is correlated with both official crime risk and fear; actors are more afraid when they sense a greater likelihood of potential criminal risk.

Despite the strong link between perceived risk and fear of crime, the risk interpretation model also allows for other variables to influence fear. Actors' judgments and emotional reactions are not made in a social vacuum. Rather, ecological and personal characteristics contextualize the process of interpreting victimization potentials and experiences. To quote Herbert Blumer (1969): "human beings act toward things on the basis of the meanings that the things have for them" (p. 2). Some things which seem like common sense are shown not to be. One might assume that direct or personal victimization might be more likely than indirect victimization to constrain behavior. That is not the case, however, for we find that indirect victimization has a stronger effect on constrained behavior than does direct victimization.

It is hoped that the application of the risk interpretation model here will spur future investigators to simultaneously consider perceived risk as an independent variable in predicting fear. The risk interpretation model specified two outcomes, fear and constrained behavior, and explained about half of the variance in each. Comparing the explained variance for these results with those from studies which omit perceived risk shows that the risk interpretation model explains more of the variance in fear and constrained behavior (e.g., Liska and Baccaglini 1990; Moeller 1989). Thus, these results appear to be an improvement over those from many previous studies. Nonetheless, I welcome investigators to attempt to confirm, refute, or modify the model. While it appears to offer a useful improvement for studying the subject, it is a model and one that needs replication.

The effects of most of the ecological variables in the model were not nearly as large as the personal variables; indeed much of the effect of the ecological variables on fear of crime was indirect. For example, neighborhood incivility clearly shapes perceived risk of crime but its direct effect on fear of crime is weak. This research included official crime risk in the form of county crime rates and found that higher personal crime rates are associated with higher fear of personal crime but that no such link was found between property crime risk and fear of property crime. Beyond the crime rates considered in this research, it would be intriguing for future research to also integrate other ecological variables which may influence fear of crime. Using the routine activities approach to predicting the occurrence of crime, previous research has shown the utility of ecological indicators of criminal motivation (e.g., unemployment rate) and criminal opportunity (e.g., proportion dwelling in multiple family housing; see Cohen and Felson 1979; Stahura and Sloan 1988). No study has specified a fairly comprehensive set of such indicators for predicting fear of crime. Although the personal variables may still well explain the bulk of the variance in fear of crime, other ecological variables merit consideration.[4]

This research also adds to our stock of knowledge by showing the importance of specifying to potential respondents what is meant by crime. Relationships between ecological, neighborhood, and personal variables vary by the type of crime considered. If respondents are only told to consider "crime," it is likely they will envision, and hence report on, violent or personal crime. If personal crime is the object of study, then the global "crime" indicator may be useful albeit still quite crude. Even among the forms of personal crime, there are important differences in how respondents judge their risk and report their fear of murder, rape, robbery, and assault. It would be most useful in subsequent research to further probe the differences across the different types of crime.

To go one step further, it appears that trying to assess various types of victimization would increase our likelihood of understanding not only each type but also important relationships with predictor variables. For instance, in the discussion of women's greater fear of crime, it was revealed that fear of sexual assault influences fear of nonsexual crime. In tests of the magnitude of such effects, fear of sexual assault showed greater or lesser effects on specific forms of nonsexual crime. The types of victimization for which fear of sexual assault had the strongest effects were those which explicitly involved face-to-face contact. There is a need to test whether fear of sexual assault shadows other types of crime which do not involve personal contact. The present survey asked about being cheated or swindled out of money—but it would be even better to ask about such con jobs done through the mail as well as those done through door-to-door contact. We would hypothesize that the effect of fear of sexual assault on fear of mail-order fraud would be far less than on door-to-door fraud schemes, and probably nonsignificant.

The findings from this survey also debunked a myth common in much fear of crime research. The myth in question concerns the "rampant fear of crime among older people." While some older adults are indeed quite fearful of crime, the evidence from this survey is that fear of most types of crime is greatest among the youngest respondents. This is the case generally speaking, and especially so for selected offenses such as burglary, rape, murder, and assault. Age differences among people twenty-five years of age or older are small, even trivial, for most types of crime. What is clear is that the people under twenty-five are the ones who are much more afraid of crime. There is some evidence to suggest that the way the questions are asked has given way to the myth of elders being prisoners of fear. It appears that the more abstract and ambiguous the questions used to measure fear of crime, the more likely that older people will score high on them (Ferraro and LaGrange 1988; LaGrange and Ferraro 1987). If questions regarding fear of crime are specific and detailed, then most findings show inverse relationships between age and fear (see also Warr 1984). In some cases the relationship is more of a reverse-j shape, with the youngest respondents showing much higher fear, and older adults manifesting slightly more fear than those in late middle age but far less than the youngest respondents.

This investigation has also shown that although age has received tremendous attention by researchers of fear of crime, the effects of gender are much more substantial and appear consistently regardless of the type of crime considered. Women are more afraid of all types of crime. When separating sexual assault from other types of crime—what may be considered nonsexual crime— it was discovered that women's fear of nonsexual crime is strongly shaped by their fear of rape. In other words, women are more afraid of crime but the fear derives primarily from the fear of sexual assault attendant with many forms of victimization. Women, especially younger women, are more afraid of sexual crime and this fear shadows daily interaction and fear of other types of victimization. We need more research on fear of sexual assault, especially research that will treat it as both an independent and dependent variable.

In addition to the research suggestions identified thus far, a few others are in order. The present study is the first to use national data to examine perceived risk and fear of a set of specific victimizations. The findings indicate that there are clear regional differences in how people judge risk, constrain behavior, and report fear. Therefore, additional research using national data sets may well enable us to specify the ecological context of coping with crime. Such an endeavor may be premature at this point but it is clear that Southerners judge their risk of crime to be higher and are more likely to take defensive actions such as adding locks to their homes and keeping a weapon available (Bankston and Thompson 1989). Future research needs to consider regional differences in how risks are interpreted in order to further reconcile the extant findings on fear of crime.

Fear of crime may well be ripe for some cross-national research. There are numerous studies of the United States, Canada, and England but cross-national comparisons are virtually nonexistent (Gomme 1986). Again, if there is a culture of coping with crime, as suggested by the studies within each nation, then identifying the differences across nations may help us better understand the etiology of fear of crime.

In addition to the call for further tests on a wider array of victimizations, the literature would also benefit from experiments on question-order, question-wording, and data collection methods. Crime is a sensitive topic to be covered in questionnaires or interview schedules. We know little about how the order of questions and the topics probed may shape findings in the various modes of data collection. As more and more researchers turn to batteries of victimization for assessing perceived risk and fear of crime, how does placement of these items affect other responses? The possibility of funnel effects is often greater when sensitive topics are queried (Schuman and Presser 1981).

Added attention to media effects may also be a propitious avenue of research. Earlier I articulated how macrostructural and ecological forces affect interpretations and micro-level processes. These micro-level processes, in turn, act back on and modify existing macrostructural properties. In other words, crime prevalence and community traits affect perceived risk, behavioral adaptations, and fear but these personal and interpersonal phenomena eventually act back on community traits and crime prevalence as evidenced in media reports and community organization. To better understand the dialectical processes between micro and macro forces, it may be useful to give added attention to media effects. Specifically, how do media portrayals and media exposure affect the risk interpretation process? These questions appear worthy of further investigation.

Finally, and perhaps most important, we know little about how fear of crime, validly and reliably measured, has changed over time. While cohort data exist for the GSS and NCS surveys, the limitations of the measures collected dampens enthusiasm for attempting to delineate change. It may be a useful task to mine those cohort data but even more important would be to study cohort and panel data on more valid and reliable indicators of fear of crime. Cohort studies would be another way to test the "aging" effects so often assessed as age differences as well as to assess social change. Panel data, where individual respondents were followed over time, would be even more powerful in assessing social and personal change. The present study represents only one "snapshot" in time; as such, I have purposefully avoided references to age changes. The task regarding age was to identify which age categories are most afraid. Next, we need to know how much of the age differences are due to aging, cohort, and period effects.

When it comes to change in the phenomena of perceived risk and fear of crime, panel studies which inquired about direct and indirect victimization could also help us see how such events constrain behavior. The time since the event and the details of the victimization experience should be assessed in order to maximize our understanding of how the victimization shapes fear. The concept of vulnerability is one that has received considerable attention in the victimology literature. Yet, most studies of reduced vulnerability are based on *post hoc* approaches. If a sufficiently large panel of subjects was followed over time, the possibility for procuring "before and after" measures of risk and fear on an adequate number of cases becomes quite plausible. Longitudinal data are not the panacea for all the shortcomings of research in the area but they represent a most promising avenue for future investigations. Hopefully, time will show that fear of crime will decline in modern societies. Yet, as long as crime rates are high, risk interpretation will continue to be part of daily life, and some citizens will be afraid.

APPENDIX A:
METHODS FOR THE FEAR OF
CRIME IN AMERICA SURVEY

SAMPLING

The *Fear of Crime in America Survey* was conducted via telephone interviews by the Public Opinion Laboratory (POL) at Northern Illinois University during January and February, 1990. The POL national sample frame is based on a multistage cluster design, structured so that each adult in the United States living in a household with a telephone has an equal chance of being selected for the sample. The sample is designed to produce 150 primary sampling units (PSUs) to maximize heterogeneity among sampling units and reduce sampling error. The Public Opinion Laboratory's 150 PSU sample is among the largest in the United States.

The total population was divided by 150 (the number of primary sampling units) which produced a sampling interval of 1,471,753. Twenty-six Standard Metropolitan Statistical Areas (SMSAs) are larger than the sampling interval and are included in the sample as self-weighting units. The twenty-six SMSAs include a population of 76,838,644. The remaining 143,924,278 cases were then divided by 124 (the remaining number of sampling units) and a new sampling interval of 1,160,680 was determined. Seven additional SMSAs are larger than this sampling interval and they are included in the sample as self-weighting units, making a total of thirty-three self-weighting PSUs in the sample. The residual population of 134,997,771 was then divided by 117 (the remaining number of PSUs) and a new sampling interval of 1,153,287 was determined. No SMSA or county exceeds this sampling interval and the remaining 117 PSUs are selected from an alphabetical listing of SMSAs and counties on a probability-proportionate-to-size basis.

The proportion of households selected in each PSU was determined by a two-step process. The thirty-three self-weighting PSUs represent 38.6 percent of the total population of the United States and these PSUs were assigned a weight proportionate to their share of the total adult population. For the non-self-weighting PSUs, the remaining proportion of cases (.612) was divided by 117 (the number of non-self-weighting PSUs), with the result that each of the non-self-weighting PSUs accounts for .52 percent of the total cases in the national sample.

The product of the probability that any given SMSA or county was selected, the probability that a given household was selected, and the probability that any given individual within a household was in the sample are essentially equal for all adults in the United States. The primary bias in the sample is that some individuals do not have telephones, although Census data indicate that this group is only about 4 percent and is a highly transient population that would have been difficult to sample by any other method.

Given the sample design described above and the known bias in the distribution of telephones among the adult population, it was necessary to calculate a weight for each case to assure that the national mix of respondents reflects the major demographic dimensions of the American population.

The weighting procedure involves three steps. First, it was necessary to correct for differential response rates across PSUs. The second step of the weighting process involved an adjustment for household size. Finally, it was necessary to adjust to known parameters for age, gender, race, and education. The distribution of telephones and of participation rates over these four demographic dimensions is biased in favor of females and better educated respondents. To make an appropriate correction, the POL utilized the most recent data from the Current Population Survey (CPS) for this study and constructed a sixty-cell matrix that reflected age, gender, race, and education. The second stage weighted sample was then distributed within the 60-cell matrix and compared to the CPS proportions. Final weights were then calculated to produce a weighted sample that accurately reflects the population of the United States, adjusted for age, gender, race, and education.

Within each household, one respondent was randomly selected. After the introductory explanation of the purpose of the survey, the interviewer asked how many persons eighteen years of age or older were regular residents of the household. The interviewer then asked for the ages of each adult, from oldest to youngest. Because all interviews were conducted on a computer-assisted-telephone-interviewing system (EQ^{tm}, Electronic Questionnaire), the number of adults and the ages of each adult were entered, and a random number generator selected the respondent within the household to be interviewed.

A final sample of 1,101 respondents was obtained with a response rate of 61 percent. This sample approximates the national noninstitutionalized population across several key variables (55% women, 84% White) but has a somewhat higher proportion of metropolitan residents (84% in this sample compared to 77% for the population; U.S. Bureau of the Census, 1989).

INTERVIEW DESIGN

The interview schedule was developed to gather the information necessary to test a risk interpretation model of fear of crime. The interview, presented as Appendix C, consisted of approximately seventy questions. Interviews averaged about fifteen minutes in duration, ranging from ten to thirty minutes. (Appendix C also includes descriptive statistics). The first question was seen as a "warm-up" item and the demographic questions at the end are placed there to provide a "cooling-off" function (Frey, 1983). In accord with advice on general interview format, the focal endogenous variables, which are the fear of crime questions, are asked early on, as numbers five through fourteen. These questions, as well as the ones on risk, are very similar to those used by Warr (1984, 1990; Warr and Stafford, 1983) but have been adapted slightly to be used in a telephone interview (Warr used a self-administered questionnaire). The interview schedule for the present research was pretested before contacting respondents for the national sample.

While Warr used an eleven-point response scale (zero to ten), I use a ten-point scale (one to ten) based upon the POL's experience in asking these types of questions. I have consulted with Warr (by telephone on September 1, 1988) regarding instrumentation of the fear and risk items and their relative placement in the interview schedule. In his experience with these items in surveys of both Seattle and Dallas, he has found that the items yield fairly consistent results regardless of their placement in the question-naire. He recommends against asking the fear and risk items immediately after one another so that respondents do not try to recall their answer for fear on an item when answering the risk question. Accordingly, we have five questions between each series of victimizations. Warr also advocates placing the fear items "first" because they are the primary items of interest. In a pretesting exercise, he found, however, that reversing the relative order of fear and risk was inconsequential.

APPENDIX B:
DESCRIPTIVE STATISTICS AND INTERVIEW SCHEDULE FOR THE FEAR OF CRIME IN AMERICA SURVEY

(Numbers in parentheses are %; some may not add to 100
due to rounding)

Hello, my name is _____ calling from the Public Opinion Laboratory at Northern Illinois University. We are conducting an important study of how people perceive crime in their local community. All responses are confidential and you don't have to answer any question you don't want to.

Now, to assure a representative cross-section of people, I need to know how many people over 17 years of age live in your household, including yourself. How many are there? ___

[Follow routine in Electronic Questionnaire (EQ^{tm}) through the selection procedure. Either obtain selected respondent or schedule recall time. Repeat introduction if a second party is the designated respondent.] Questions 1–3 are for identifying the respondent.

We are calling several hundred people whose telephone numbers have been randomly selected. There are some important questions I would like to ask you which should only take a few minutes. We're a university-based organization, so your answers will be kept confidential. Feel free to ask questions at any time, and you may withhold a response to any item you wish. Okay?

4. First of all, do you belong to a neighborhood or community "crime watch" program? 1. (12%) yes 2. (88%) no

At one time or another, most of us have experienced fear about becoming the victim of crime. Some crimes probably frighten you more than others. We are interested in *how afraid* people are in everyday life of being a victim of different kinds of crimes. Please rate your fear on a scale of 1 to ten where 1 means you are NOT AFRAID AT ALL and ten means you are VERY AFRAID.

First, rate your fear of . . . (*read item*) . . .   *Record Number*
                                                              (1–10)
                                                              (mean)

5. Being approached on the street by a beggar or panhandler.   2.9
6. Please rate your fear of being cheated, conned, or swindled out of your money.   3.7
7. . . . having someone break into your home while you are away.   5.7
8. . . . having someone break into you home while you are there.   5.0
9. . . . being raped or sexually assaulted.   4.4
10. . . . being murdered.   4.5
11. . . . being attacked by someone with a weapon?   5.1
12. . . . having your car stolen.   4.5
13. . . . being robbed or mugged on the street.   4.4
14. . . . having your property damaged by vandals.   4.6
15. How safe do you feel out alone in your neighborhood during the day? Do you feel . . .
    1. (77%) very safe   3. (3%) somewhat unsafe
    2. (19%) somewhat safe   4. (2%) very unsafe?
                                  X = mean = 1.3

16. *Split ballot: forms a and b divided among sample.*
    A. How safe do you feel out alone in your neighborhood at night? Do you feel . . .
    1. (38%) very safe   3. (14%) somewhat unsafe
    2. (39%) somewhat safe   4. (9%) very unsafe
                                  X = 1.9

    B. How safe do you feel out alone in your neighborhood at night, say between sunset and ten o'clock?
    1. (48%) very safe   3. (12%) somewhat unsafe
    2. (35%) somewhat safe   4. (5%) very unsafe
                                  X = 1.7

17. Is there any area right around there—that is, within a mile—where you would be afraid to walk alone at night?
    1. (44%) yes   2. (56%) no

18. How safe from crime do you feel inside your home during the day?
    1. (82%) very safe   3. (1%) somewhat unsafe
    2. (17%) somewhat safe   4. (1%) very unsafe
                      $X = 1.2$

19. How safe from crime do you feel inside your home during the night?
    1. (58%) very safe   3. (7%) somewhat unsafe
    2. (34%) somewhat safe   4. (2%) very unsafe
                      $X = 1.5$

You have already rated your fear of different kinds of crimes, now I want you to rate THE CHANCE THAT A SPECIFIC THING WILL HAPPEN TO YOU DURING THE COMING YEAR. On a scale from 1 to ten where 1 means it's not at all likely and ten means it's very likely—how LIKELY do you think it is that you will . . . *(read item)* . . .

                                    Record Number
                                     (1–10)

20. . . . be approached on the street by a beggar or panhandler?   4.1

21. . . . be cheated, conned, or swindled out of some money?   3.8

22. . . . have someone attempt to break into your home while you are away?   3.9

23. . . . have someone break into your home while you are there?   2.5

24. . . . be raped or sexually assaulted?   2.3

25. . . . be murdered?   2.1

26. . . . be attacked by someone with a weapon?   2.6

27. . . . have your car stolen?   3.7

28. . . . be robbed or mugged on the street?   3.0

29. . . . have your property damaged by vandals?   3.6

30. In the past year, have you been the victim of any crime?
    1. (19%) yes   2. (81%) no

31. Please tell me what crime or crimes you were the victim of in the past year:

Crime (*write in*)

_____

_____

_____

32. In the past year, has a close friend or relative of yours been the victim of a crime?

1. (31%) yes   2. (70%) no

Now I will mention a few things that people sometimes consider to be problems in their local neighborhood. After I read each item, please tell me HOW SERIOUS a problem it is in YOUR neighborhood by indicating whether it's not a problem, somewhat of a problem, or a very serious problem.

HOW GREAT A PROBLEM IS . . . (*read item*) . . .

	Not a Problem	Somewhat of a Problem	Very Serious Problem
33. . . . Trash and litter lying around your neighborhood	(66%) 1	(27%) 2	(7%) 3 X = 1.4
34. . . . Neighborhood dogs running loose	(62%) 1	(31%) 2	(8%) 3 X = 1.5
35. . . . Inconsiderate or disruptive neighbors	(75%) 1	(20%) 2	(6%) 3 X = 1.3
36. . . . Graffiti on sidewalks and walls	(87%) 1	(10%) 2	(3%) 3 X = 1.2
37. . . . Vacant houses and unkempt lots	(81%) 1	(16%) 2	(3%) 3 X = 1.2
38. . . . Unsupervised youth	(62%) 1	(29%) 2	(9%) 3 X = 1.5
39. . . . Too much noise	(78%) 1	(18%) 2	(4%) 3 X = 1.3
40. . . . People drunk or high on drugs in public	(74%) 1	(19%) 2	(8%) 3 X = 1.3
41. . . . Abandoned cars or car parts lying around	(84%) 1	(13%) 2	(3%) 3 X = 1.2

42. If you had a problem, could you rely on your nearby neighbors for help?
    1. (88%) yes   2. (7%) no   3. (5%) not sure   X = 1.2

43. Do you feel like you are a part of your neighborhood, or do you feel like you don't belong?
    1. (86%) a part   2. (8%) don't belong   3. (6%) not sure
                                                    X = 1.2

44. Think of the people who live in the four houses nearest you. If they were all to move away in the next year, how many of them would you really miss?
    1. (28%) none   4. (10%) three of them
    2. (16%) one of them   5. (24%) all of them   X = 2.9
    3. (23%) two of them

45. Do you see strangers in your neighborhood . . .
    1. (16%) very often   2. (46%) occasionally
                           3. (39%) almost never   X = 2.2

46. Are you aware of any crime committed in your neighborhood during the past year?
    1. (43%) yes, ask #47
    2. (51%) no, skip to #48

47. Do you think most of the crime was committed by people who live or work there or by strangers?
    1. (36%) people in neighborhood
            657 cases missing—no crime in neighborhood
    2. (64%) strangers

Now I'd like to read a list of activities some people do to reduce their risk to crime. For each one, please tell me if you have done it. Have you . . .

48. . . . Engraved ID numbers
    on your possessions?   1. (34%) yes   2. (66%) no
49. . . . Installed extra locks
    on windows or doors?   1. (57%) yes   2. (43%) no
50. . . . Bought a watchdog?   1. (25%) yes   2. (76%) no
51. . . . Kept a weapon in your
    home for protection?   1. (41%) yes   2. (59%) no
52. . . . Added outside lighting? 1. (58%) yes   2. (43%) no

53. . . . Learned more
about self-defense?   1. (38%) yes   2. (62%) no
54. . . . Started carrying
something to defend yourself? 1. (19%) yes   2. (81%) no
55. Do you generally avoid
unsafe areas during the day
because of crime?   1. (52%) yes   2. (48%) no
56. Do you avoid unsafe areas
during the night
because of crime?   1. (75%) yes   2. (25%) no
57. Within the past year,
have you limited or
changed your daily activities
because of crime?   1. (14%) yes   2. (87%) no

Finally, I have just a few more questions to help us make comparisons among the groups of people we have talked to.

58. How long have you lived at your present address?
    11.4 number of years

59. What is your zip code? _____   % urban = 84.4

60. Do you live in . . .
    1. (75%) a single family house   4. (3%) a condominium
    2. (14%) an apartment   5. (3%) a trailer home
    3. (4%) a duplex   6. (.1%) a rooming house
                                      7. (2%) or what?
                                          if other, ask #61

61. What type of home do you live in?

    _____

62. How many children, under the age of 18, live in your
    household?   X = .83

63. In what year were you born? 1945.7   Average age = 44.3

64. What ethnic group do you belong/identify with?
1. (85%) white   3. (4%) Hispanic
2. (8%) black   4. (3%) other, ask #65

65. What ethnic group do you belong/identify with?

    _____

66. How much schooling have you completed?
   1. (10%) grade school   4. (21%) college grad   X = 2.9
   2. (31%) H.S. graduate   5. (10%) postgrad
   3. (30%) some college

67. Generally speaking, would you describe your present health as . . .
   1. (42%) excellent   3. (12%) fair
   2. (44%) good   4. (2%) poor   X = 1.7

68. And would you say your health has in the past three years . . .
   1. (29%) improved   3. (60%) stayed the same   X = 2.3
   2. (11%) declined

69. *(IF YOU ARE NOT SURE, ASK THEM IF THEY ARE MALE OR FEMALE)*
   1. (45%) male   2. (55%) female

   Asked only of subsample:
   70. How tall are you? 67.1 inches
   71. And how much do you weigh? 159.3 pounds

THAT COMPLETES OUR SURVEY.
I WOULD LIKE TO THANK YOU VERY MUCH
FOR TAKING THE TIME TO TALK WITH ME.
HAVE A GOOD DAY/EVENING.

Record respondent's phone number: (   )

Interviewer's name _____

This research was completed at Northern Illinois University and Purdue University with support from the AARP Andrus Foundation. Data were collected during January and February, 1990 by the Public Opinion Laboratory at NIU, DeKalb, IL 60115

APPENDIX C:
SUPPLEMENTARY TABLES

Table C–1
Correlations Among the 10 Fear of Victimization Items[a]

	1	2	3	4	5	6	7	8	9
1. Beggar	1.0								
2. Con	.41	1.0							
3. Burglary-Away	.38	.48	1.0						
4. Burglary-Home	.32	.42	.67	1.0					
5. Sexual Assault	.37	.36	.48	.69	1.0				
6. Murder	.31	.42	.47	.69	.72	1.0			
7. Attack	.34	.41	.53	.68	.67	.81	1.0		
8. Car Theft	.35	.42	.49	.36	.30	.37	.47	1.0	
9. Robbery/Mugging	.45	.46	.52	.55	.59	.64	.72	.55	1.0
10. Vandalism	.36	.40	.49	.38	.34	.37	.44	.48	.53

[a]All Pearson correlation coefficients in the matrix are significant ($p < .01$).

Table C–2
Correlations Among the 10 Perceived Risk of Victimization Items[a]

	1	2	3	4	5	6	7	8	9
1. Beggar	1.0								
2. Con	.33	1.0							
3. Burglary-Away	.24	.29	1.0						
4. Burglary-Home	.21	.24	.64	1.0					
5. Sexual Assault	.18	.22	.49	.63	1.0				
6. Murder	.26	.24	.50	.62	.66	1.0			
7. Attack	.33	.29	.51	.60	.58	.76	1.0		
8. Car Theft	.28	.30	.45	.33	.33	.32	.42	1.0	
9. Robbery/Mugging	.38	.33	.52	.54	.60	.59	.68	.50	1.0
10. Vandalism	.28	.31	.45	.41	.38	.37	.44	.41	.47

[a]All Pearson correlation coefficients in the matrix are significant (p < .01).

Table C–3
Operational Definition of Variables to Predict Perceived Risk[a]

I. Ecological Characteristics

A. Crime rates—offenses known to the police as reported by the UCR.
Crime (overall): sum of murder, rape, robbery, assault, burglary, auto theft (alpha = .87).
Personal crime: sum of murder, rape, robbery, assault (alpha = .70).
Property crime: sum of robbery, burglary, motor vehicle theft (alpha = .94).

B. Region: midwest, south, west, and northeast as defined by UCR; binary codes for each (0,1).

C. Community type: metropolitan (1), nonmetropolitan (0).

II. Neighborhood Perceptions[b]

A. Incivility: Now I will mention a few things that people sometimes consider to be problems in their local neighborhood. After I read each item, please tell me *how serious* a problem it is in *your* neighborhood by indicating whether it's not a problem, somewhat of a problem, or a very serious problem.
How great a problem is . . .
   1. Trash and litter lying around your neighborhood?
   2. Neighborhood dogs running loose?
   3. Inconsiderate or disruptive neighbors?
   4. Graffiti on sidewalks and walls?
   5. Vacant houses and unkept lots?
   6. Unsupervised youth?
   7. Too much noise?
   8. People drunk or high on drugs in public?
   9. Abandoned cars or car parts lying around?

Items were asked in above order. Eight items (item 4 excluded) are summed for the general incivility index (alpha = .77). Items 3, 6, 7, and 8 are summed for the social incivility index (alpha = .72). Items 1, 2, 5, and 9 were summed for the physical incivility index (alpha = .63). A latent variable was specified for incivility treating the social and physical indexes as the measured variables. The lambda (y) coefficients for the two indicators are .76 and .65 respectively.

B. Cohesion: A latent variable of the following items was created.
1. If you had a problem, could you rely on your nearby neighbors for help? (1 = yes, 0 = otherwise).
2. Do you feel like you are a part of your neighborhood, or do you feel like you don't belong? (1 = a part, 0 = otherwise).

Table C–3 (continued)

3. Think of the people who live in the four houses nearest you. If they were all to move away in the next year, how many of them would you really miss? (4 = all of them, 0 = none).
The lambda coefficients for the three indicators are .51, .67, and .50 respectively.
C. Crime watch: Watch present in respondent's neighborhood (1), otherwise (0).

III. Personal Characteristics

A. Age: Years since birth.
B. Gender: Women (1), men (0).
C. Race: Nonwhite (1), white (0).
D. Education: Schooling completed (5 = post graduate, 1 = grade school).
E. Health: Self-assessed health (4 = excellent, 1 = poor)
F. Housing Tenure: Years in current residence (6 = 31+ years, 1 = 1 or fewer years).
G. Victimization (Direct): In the past year, have you been the victim of any crime? (1 = yes, 0 = no).
H. Indirect Victimization: In the past year, has a close friend or relative of yours been the victim of a crime? (1 = yes, 0 = no).

[a]See Appendix B for survey instrument that displays all response categories.
[b]Information on using the items as simple additive indexes (or subindexes) is provided as a convenience for the reader although the latent variables derived from them are used in the analyses presented here.

Table C–4
Correlations Among Replication Items and Indexes of Fear and Risk of Crime[a]

	Fear	Risk	NCS-D	NCS-N	GSS
Fear Index	1.0				
Risk Index	.56	1.0			
NCS-Day	.33	.42	1.0		
NCS-Night	.43	.51	.64	1.0	
GSS	.29	.30	.25	.49	1.0

[a]All correlations are significant (p<.01).

Table C–5
Means and Standard Deviations for Victimization Fear
and Perceived Risk by Sex

Type of Fear	Men		Women	
	Mean	*SD*	*Mean*	*SD*
Beggar	2.36	± 1.86	3.36	± 2.57**
Cheat/Con	3.40	± 2.56	3.89	± 2.90**
Burglary/Away	5.18	± 2.82	6.18	± 2.98**
Burglary/Home	3.85	± 2.97	5.90	± 3.42**
Sexual Assault	2.21	± 2.47	6.09	± 3.36**
Murder	3.48	± 3.05	5.30	± 3.67**
Attack	4.31	± 2.92	5.69	± 3.40**
Car Theft	4.25	± 2.79	4.76	± 2.90**
Robbery/Mugging	3.66	± 2.54	5.05	± 3.16**
Vandalism	4.31	± 2.58	4.89	± 2.95**
Fear (total)	37.02	± 18.41	51.22	± 23.25**
Personal Fear[b]	-1.36	± 2.67	1.12	± 3.57**
Property Fear	-.55	± 2.41	.44	± 2.76**
Type of Risk				
Beggar	4.54	± 3.48	3.83	± 3.31**
Cheat/Con	4.08	± 2.90	3.60	± 2.78**
Burglary/Away	3.55	± 2.29	4.20	± 2.57**
Burglary/Home	2.07	± 1.77	2.79	± 2.21**
Sexual Assault	1.38	± 1.03	2.98	± 2.33**
Murder	1.80	± 1.64	2.27	± 2.19**
Attack	2.38	± 1.85	2.76	± 2.34**
Car Theft	3.60	± 2.43	3.79	± 2.66
Robbery/Mugging	2.66	± 1.98	3.21	± 2.51**
Vandalism	3.37	± 2.34	3.72	± 2.75*
Risk (total)	29.34	± 13.84	33.26	± 17.98**

Table C-5 (continued)

Type of Risk	Mean		SD	Mean		SD
Personal Risk[b]	-.75	±	2.19	.62	±	3.50**
Property Risk	-.25	±	2.15	.21	±	2.53**

[a]Differences tested by t-test of means.
[b]The personal and property dimensions of fear and risk are latent constructs derived from confirmatory factor analysis. As standard normal variables, with a mean of zero, men manifest negative values while women manifest positive values.
**$p \leq .01$.
*$p \leq .05$.

Table C–6
Predicting Fear of Nonsexual Crime Among Women (N = 554)

Independent Variables	Model I	Model II
ECOLOGICAL		
Official Crime (nonsexual)	-.00[a]*	-.00
	-.08[b]	-.05
South[c]	-2.72	-1.38
	-.06	-.04
West	-.71	-.93
	-.01	-.02
Northeast	2.32	-.91
	.05	-.02
Urban	3.08	1.44
	.05	.03
NEIGHBORHOOD		
Incivility	-.80	.01
	-.05	.00
Crime Watch	.18	-1.35
	.00	-.02
PERSONAL		
Age	-.65**	-.39*
	-.55	-.33
Age^2	.01*	.00*
	.51	.37
Race (nonwhite)	4.00	2.73
	.07	.05
Education	-1.70*	-1.02
	-.09	-.05
Health	.35	-.74
	.01	-.03
Housing Tenure	-.30	-.03
	-.02	-.00

Table C–6 (continued)

Victimization	-.69	-2.74
	-.01	-.05
Indirect Victimization	3.02	2.00
	.07	.05
Perceived Risk (nonsexual)	.60**	.74**
	.46	.58
Constrained Behavior	4.07**	1.60
	.14	.05
RAPE		
Official Rape Rate		.00
		.05
Fear of Rape		3.90**
		.62
Intercept	42.94	32.32
R^2	.32	.67

[a]Unstandardized coefficient.
[b]Standardized coefficient.
[c]Midwest serves as the reference group for the regional comparisons.
*$p \leq .05$.
**$p \leq .01$.

NOTES

CHAPTER 1. WHITHER FEAR OF CRIME?

1. On the other hand, functionalists have long argued that crime and the reaction to it may latently increase social solidarity. Yet, when *fear* of crime is prevalent, there is little evidence to date that social integration increases (Conklin 1975; Liska and Warner 1991).

CHAPTER 2. INTERPRETING CRIMINAL REALITIES: "RISKY BUSINESS"

1. Other studies which do not consider risk or perceived risk of crime include, but are not limited to: Braungart, Braungart, and Hoyer (1980); Clarke and Lewis (1982); Clemente and Kleiman (1976); Cutler (1980); Jeffords (1983); Kennedy and Krahn (1984); Kennedy and Silverman (1985); Lebowitz (1975); Norton and Courlander (1982); Pollack and Patterson (1980).

2. Other studies which explicitly consider risk or perceived risk of crime include, but are not limited to: Janson and Ryder (1983); LaGrange and Ferraro (1989); LaGrange, Ferraro, and Supancic (1992); Lawton and Yaffe (1980); Miethe and Lee (1984); Ortega and Myles (1987); Stafford and Galle (1984); Warr and Stafford (1983).

3. Symbolic interactionism posits an alternative to the two well-known positions regarding the genesis of the meaning of things. The first widely held position is found in the philosophy of realism, which asserts that meaning is to be considered intrinsic to the object. Meaning is, therefore, a natural part of the objective makeup of a thing, and one intuitively apprehends the meaning as self-evident. The other widely held position on the epistemology of meaning is formulated upon the psychological makeup of the individual who is perceiving the object. Ultimately, meaning is a function of the psychological characteristics of the person. Blumer differs from these perspectives by stating that meaning arises "in the process of interaction between people. The meaning of a thing for a person grows out of the ways in which other persons act toward the person with regard to the thing" (Blumer 1969, p. 4).

Blumer's (1969) book contains some original (fresh) writing for that period but several chapters are reprints of works which appeared between 1939 and 1969. Thus, it may appear on the surface that I cite some of the earliest works in the development of symbolic interactionism but skip to 1969. In reality, of course, the various chapters of the 1969 book were written over a thirty-year period simultaneous to vigorous discussion and exchange regarding interactionism and role theory (Sarbin and Farberow 1952).

4. Several commentators have noted that Thomas's concept of the definition of the situation lacks specificity and is used in different ways throughout his published works (Blumer 1979; Stryker 1980; Volkhart 1951). Thomas himself also recognized that many of his ideas changed over time (see Blumer 1979, pp. 82–83). Despite these problems, Thomas's use of the definition of the situation, suggests certain definitional criteria and provides for empirical examinations of the concept (e.g., Stebbins 1969).

5. It should be noted that many sociological theories including rational-choice theory as well as psychological theories on cognition and judgmental heuristics share a common interest in interpreting risk (Singelmann 1972). Although they may differ on the process involved and the relative importance of the relevant parameters, these theories encourage us to view behavior as contingent upon actors *judging* situations, estimating the likelihood of events and consequences, and selecting a line of action which seems best, or at least acceptable, given the circumstances. For instance, in exchange theories, such judgments of risk are involved in determining what behaviors are valuable as well as in the profit-estimation process (Chadwick-Jones 1976). For the cognitive theories, one of the first steps in information processing is the assessment of the degree of risk involved in a proposed line of action (Kahneman, Slovic, and Tversky 1982; Tversky and Kahneman 1982). As Slovic, Fischhoff and Lichtenstein (1982) assert, risk assessments are "inherently subjective" and require the person to make inferences based on judgment rules, also known as heuristics. (See works by Cohrssen and Covello [1989] and Douglas [1985] for an overview of the field of risk analysis.)

6. A theoretical perspective closely related to the incivility hypothesis which could also be integrated is defensible space theory. Taylor, Gottfredson, and Brower's (1980) defensible space theory helps to explain how physical design features influence both crime and victimization reactions by affecting territorial functioning and local social climate (Taylor, Gottfredson, and Brower 1984). The thrust of the theory is more oriented to how physical design may reduce crime and gives little attention to perceptions of risk. Therefore, while much of it is consistent with the incivility literature, it is not as directly relevant to the present concerns.

7. Fear of crime may also be conceptualized as a stressor affecting mental health and well-being (e.g., Ward, LaGory, and Sherman 1986) or as a determinant of community dissatisfaction (e.g., Taylor, Taub, and Peterson 1986; Taub, Taylor, and Dunham 1984). While exploring such relationships is important in its own right, it is beyond the scope of this project. Given the limitations of most of the previous research, the goal of this book is to more rigorously identify the determinants of fear of crime, with emphasis on the possible operation of perceived risk of crime. I hope to examine the consequences of fear of crime in future research.

CHAPTER 3. MEASURING RISK AND FEAR OF CRIME

1. The National Crime Survey recently underwent a name change to the National Crime Victimization Survey. Because the studies most often referred to here used the NCS—prior to 1991—I use the traditional name. Among the studies using the NCS measure or something very close to it are: Balkin (1979); Baumer (1985); Garofalo (1979); Kennedy and Krahn (1984); Kennedy and Silverman (1985); Liska et al. (1982); Liska and Warner (1991); Maxfield (1984); Riger et al. (1978); Taylor et al. (1984); Yin (1982).

Among the studies using the GSS measure or something very close to it are: Braungart et al. (1980); Clarke and Lewis (1982); Clemente and Kleiman (1976, 1977); Cutler (1980); DeFronzo (1979); Jeffords (1983); Lebowitz (1975).

2. The emotional *experience* of fear during survey data collection may not materialize when asking about burglary in one's home; but it would become manifest if one was held at gunpoint in one's home by masked robbers. Given that most people never face many crime situations, there will be tremendous difficulty in actually gathering true fear reactions to various types of crime. Because survey data are removed in time and space from the actual fear-producing event, they are expressions of the imaginative rehearsal of such events.

3. There are dozens of other studies which do not measure risk or perceived risk of crime while purportedly studying fear of crime (for examples, see, Braungart, Braungart, and Hoyer 1980; Clarke and Lewis 1982; Clemente and Kleiman 1976; Jeffords 1983; Kennedy and Krahn 1984; Kennedy and Silverman 1985; Lebowitz 1975; Norton and Courlander 1982; Parker 1988; Parker and Ray 1990; Pollack and Patterson 1980).

4. For instance, Lawton and Yaffe (1980), which have very respectable measures of fear of crime, report a standardized effect of.21 for offi-

cial risk on fear with other variables such as community size and victimization having slightly stronger effects.

5. Riger et al. (1978) also present one table using the national NCS data to introduce the problem of higher fear among women. The bulk of their analysis, however, is derived from their survey of 68 men and 299 women from Chicago, Philadelphia, and San Francisco. See also Riger and Gordon (1981).

6. Indeed, Randy LaGrange and I had tried a trichotomous response category in a smaller-scale project (LaGrange and Ferraro 1989) and felt the 10-point scale was an improvement on several fronts.

7. Although OLS could have been used for the confirmatory factor analysis, a maximum-likelihood analysis was undertaken. A LISREL estimation method was chosen because it gives all of the essential information derived from an OLS factor analysis and enables one to *(a)* compare the OLS estimates with alternative models and *(b)* discern correlated measurement errors (Joreskog and Sorbom 1988). The results of the LISREL analysis confirm that the items may be used either to create a unidimensional factor for fear, as well as one for risk, or to create a slightly different two-factor model for each (i.e., fear and risk). The suitability of the two-factor solution seems great after evaluating alternative models and goodness-of-fit statistics (i.e., chi-square per degrees of freedom, goodness-of-fit index, and root mean square residual). The goodness-of-fit statistics permit a test of whether the differences between the estimated covariance matrix and the observed covariance matrix are small enough to be sampling fluctuations (Hayduk 1987).

8. The models displayed provide an excellent fit to the data once correlated errors of measurement are accounted for in the estimation. Given that the questions used to measure these concepts are based on the same question trunk, with ten stems reflecting the victimizations, it is not surprising that correlated measurement errors exist. Indeed, baseline models without permitting correlated errors of measurement to be estimated did not have as good a fit as the ones reported here. This is often the case when social psychological indicators are being used (Bollen 1989). The improvement in fit due to estimating correlated measurement errors makes it quite unlikely that the more restrictive baseline models are correct (Bollen 1989; Hayduk 1987).

CHAPTER 4. OFFICIAL AND PERCEIVED VICTIMIZATION RISK

1. When compared to other risks such as disease, accidents, and fires, some types of criminal victimization are quite likely to happen. In comparing one year incidence of over fifteen "negative events" for

households, personal theft without contact is the event most likely to be experienced—by about 11 percent of all households (Bureau of Justice Statistics 1989, 1991). In most years, this is followed by household theft, burglary, motor vehicle injury, assault, death by any cause, motor vehicle theft, and robbery. Events with annual household incidence less than 1 percent include rape, murder, house fire, motor vehicle death, suicide, and cancer (Bureau of Justice Statistics 1989, 1991; Karmen 1991).

In sum, the incidence of the less serious forms of crime is quite high; fortunately, the incidence of the more serious crimes is much smaller. Within any given year, some households will not experience any crime, while others may be repeatedly victimized. In addition, ethnic-minority headed and urban households have overall higher rates of victimization. Households with higher incomes are more likely than others to suffer from property crime but less likely to be victimized by violent crime (Bureau of Justice Statistics 1991). While criminal victimization is clearly too high, there is some evidence of declines in household victimization over the past fifteen years. Despite the leveling off or declines in various indicators of crime, public opinion polls generally do not show any such decrease in the concern about crime (Skogan 1990; Stinchcombe et al. 1980).

2. Nevertheless, the correlation is not perfect and systematic variation has been uncovered (e.g., Pyle 1990; Pyle & Hanten 1974; Waller & Okihiro 1978; Warr 1980). McPherson (1978) found the public accurate in estimating risk of crime for personal crime but less accurate for property crime. Many scholars attribute such discrepancies to media distortion of crime (Baker, Nienstedt, Everett, & McCleary 1983; Quinney 1970). The media distortion interpretation is based on the "overemphasis on violent crime, the creation of artificial crime waves, the use of crime news as 'filler,' misleading reports of crime statistics, and police control of crime news" (Warr 1982, p. 187).

3. Interviews with people who survive an accident during train or air travel often remark that they "never thought it would happen" to them. The same mechanism is often operant when discovering illnesses such as cancer or being victimized in a violent crime.

4. We have trend data from the NCS and GSS surveys but, as detailed earlier, these are not valid measures of fear.

5. When ninth-grade boys stab a fellow Dartmouth, Massachusetts student to death and then trade high-fives and laughter, the phenomenon of crime garners more attention and, perhaps, generalized fear. Or consider when a teenager chases and overtakes a woman in Oakland, California and then commences to stab her to death. The fact that onlookers chant "Kill her! Kill her!" may spur fresh definitions of the world as an unsafe place.

6. The operational definition of violent or personal crime is identical with the UCR. The index for property crime, however, is constructed

to reflect, as closely as possible, the latent variable for perceived property risk. Note, therefore, that robbery is included in both subindexes of official crime.

CHAPTER 5. HITTING PAYDIRT WITH RISK INTERPRETATION?

1. Scenarios are based on real events but names have been changed (here and elsewhere in the book).

2. As reviewed in chapter 3, Taylor et al. (1986) treat measures of both perceived risk and fear as indicators of fear while Liska et al. (1988) simply use the two NCS measures as indicators of fear. Thus, neither paper specifies perceived risk as a separate concept to be tested. Yet, it may be argued that the entire concept of constrained behavior is predicated upon a crime risk assessment.

3. Lee (1983) also found that most types of social integration do not affect fear of crime. I also tested for indirect and total effects in preliminary models and found neighborhood cohesion to contribute little to predicting either perceived risk or fear. In addition, it was nonsignificant in equations predicting constrained behavior. The lack of effects may be due to its correlation with incivility ($r = -.21$). Social incivility is one domain of our incivility construct and is clearly related to neighborhood cohesion. Incivility appears to be the more robust predictor when comparing alternative specifications.

4. The measurement model has four constructs each of which is represented by two observed variables. The constructs and their indicators are: incivility, social (.76) and physical (.65); perceived risk, personal (.78) and property crime (.95); constrained behavior, avoidance (.58) and defensive (.31); and fear, personal (.86) and property crime (.87). The model also contains three significant correlated measurement errors (off-diagonal of theta epsilon). The adjusted goodness-of-fit index is .99 with chi square = 14.35, 9df; p = .11.

5. The full model has an adjusted goodness-of-fit index of .91 (chi square = 322.90, 70 df). Another indicator of fit with large sample size is the chi-square per degrees of freedom. This model fit falls within the 5 to 1 ratio recommended (Wheaton et al. 1977).

CHAPTER 6. ARE OLDER PEOPLE PRISONERS OF FEAR?

1. Other studies which use the NCS or GSS measures and interpret them as fear include: Baumer (1985); Braungart, Braungart, and Hoyer (1980); Clarke and Lewis (1982); Kennedy and Krahn (1984); Kennedy

and Silverman (1985); Lebowitz (1975); Lewis and Salem (1986); Liska, Lawrence, and Sanchirico (1982); Liska, Sanchirico, and Reed (1988); and Taylor, Gottfredson, and Brower (1984).

2. The question for the General Social Survey was an exact replication: "Is there any area right around there—that is, within a mile—where you would be afraid to walk alone at night?" (1) yes, (0) no. For the National Crime Survey questions, a slight modification was undertaken to eliminate the "double-barrelled" question. The question was asked in the NCS as follows: "How safe do you feel or would you feel out alone in your neighborhood during the day? Do you feel (1) very safe, (2) somewhat safe, (3) somewhat unsafe, or (4) very unsafe? The phrase "or would you feel" was omitted from the NCS questions for daytime activity (above) and the parallel question for nighttime activity.

3. Analyses in which official and perceived risk were omitted for the MCA were also performed with findings on the age relationships similar to those presented below. Multiple Classification Analysis (MCA) is a convenient method to be used for examining the net means on fear of crime while controlling for relevant covariates identified in chapter 5.

CHAPTER 7. UNRAVELING FEAR OF CRIME AMONG WOMEN

1. Despite the general robustness of the findings on sex differences, there are some intriguing exceptions. For instance, Lee (1982b) used a variety of indicators to assess fear among older men and women in the state of Washington and found sex differences on some indicators of fear, especially those which required subjects to imagine walking alone on the street at night, but no sex differences on other indicators.

2. The closest precedent in the literature that I have found is in the work of Warr (1984, 1985). He tests models where *each* crime is considered in relation to all others in what he defines as omnibus crime.

3. The variable for nonsexual crime refers to an additive index for all victimizations *except* rape. Parallel measures were created for fear and risk with Cronbach alpha coefficients of reliability equal to.91 for fear and.84 for perceived risk. For subsequent analyses, an index of official risk of nonsexual crime (excluding rape) was also created from the UCR data used here. The official risk of nonsexual crime index possesses an alpha of.90. (I want to reiterate my appreciation to JoAnn Miller, Jack W. Spencer, and Cathy Streifel for encouraging me to explore the nomenclature of sexual and nonsexual crime.)

4. To be consistent with my own work and that of others (e.g., Stafford and Galle 1984; Warr 1984), fear is interpreted as the residual of the fear measure on the perceived risk measure. Thus, it is appropriate

to not only add the fear indicator but either (a) the perceived risk and fear of rape or (b) the residual of fear of rape regressed on perceived risk of rape. I have estimated the effect both ways but choose the latter approach because of its ease in presentation and interpretation. Unstandardized residual scores are used.

5. The net means for each group were as follows: 18–24 years of age, 7.37; 25–34, 6.42; 35–44, 6.20; 45–54, 5.88; 55–64, 5.27; 65–74, 5.26; and 75+, 5.64.

6. There is also the possibility that fear of murder is implicated in fear of rape. As Gordon and Riger (1989) describe, "The threat of death during a rape attack is a very real one to many women, since women believe that on the average at least 25 percent of rape victims are killed during their attacks" (p. 9). While the actual figure is only about 3 percent, the possibility remains.

CHAPTER 8. CONSTRAINTS ON DAILY LIVING

1. It has become a social scientific ritual to claim that "previous research is limited" for understanding a subject under investigation. While this ritual may have been practiced somewhat in previous chapters, I have also argued that there is ample research to offer some conclusions in the study of fear of crime. When it comes to coping with crime, however, there are only a few solid empirical generalizations, and the general area is in dire need of fresh study. I hope not to sound ritualistic but to stimulate research on what people actually do when confronted by crime risk.

2. Logistic regression is generally recognized as statistical procedure of choice when analyzing categorical outcomes (Aldrich and Nelson 1984; Swafford 1980). It easily handles categorical and continuous independent variables and yields better estimates than linear regression or discriminant models when the outcome is highly skewed. These equations were estimated with logistic regression and OLS regression with almost identical results. The logistic regression results are presented, however, for more exact model fitting—following the advice of Cleary and Angel (1984). The explained variance for each equation presented is the pseudo R^2 presented by Aldrich and Nelson (1984).

3. It should be noted that both the effects for age and housing tenure may reflect differences in home ownership. Older adults, especially those in their eighties, often downsize their living quarters after the death of one's spouse and growing functional limitations. Therefore, some of the elders may not own pets because of restrictions on rental properties. Housing tenure also probably reflects home ownership to some degree—

people who rent will have lower scores on housing tenure—and pets are less likely to be permitted in rented housing units.

4. Following the findings of Bankston et al. (1990), a product term to reflect the interaction of south and female was created and entered into the equation for keeping a weapon in the home. The interaction term, however, was nonsignificant. Whereas Bankston et al. studied carrying a gun in Louisiana and the present study examines owning a weapon throughout the United States, it is impossible to determine why the effect of the interaction term is not the same in the two projects.

5. We did not ask if respondents owned their homes but this looks like an important consideration in future research on constrained behavior if changes to the living environment are being made.

6. Moreover, certain cities have reputations as high crime cities. Crime rates, especially violent personal crime rates, vary from cities like Indianapolis and Minneapolis, to those including Detroit and Washington, DC. For instance, Indianapolis and Minneapolis both have homicide rates under fifteen per 100,000 while Detroit and Washington have rates over sixty per 100,000 (Maguire and Flanagan 1991). This information and the more generalized reputations enter into decisions about daily activities, travel, and relocation. The perceptions are not always accurate but shape the actor's world nonetheless (Gould and White 1974; Smith and Patterson 1990). New York, for example, has a homicide rate half that of Atlanta but it would be seen as a more dangerous city to most Americans.

CHAPTER 9. SCIENCE AND CIVILITY: IMPLICATIONS FROM RISK INTERPRETATION

1. It would be foolish to fall into a "world we have lost" syndrome. History is filled with human atrocities: feeding Christians to lions and Jews to Nazi gas chambers, lynching Black men, and women pickling the ears of outlaws who were outgunned. Still the *structure* of moral activity is fundamentally different in pluralistic societies (Erikson 1966).

2. The fact that the normative order is so relative and rife with change further accelerates social change. As Peter Berger (1963, p. 130) stated, "Nonrecognition and counter-definition of social norms are always potentially revolutionary." Social systems traverse cycles of organization, disorganization, and reorganization. It is unclear what will happen to the pivotal moral debates over which America and other modern societies have struggled during the past thirty years. Unless convergence on the definition of these acts emerges across the mainstream, it would appear that the moral reliability of the nation will continue to be weak.

Could it also be that our justice system, which is devoted to curbing criminal victimization, latently functions—at least in part—to propagate the very phenomena it seeks to suspend? The ancient legal systems that gave way to Western law viewed crime largely in terms of its impact on victims, their families, and communities. This changed during the Middle Ages when England started covering what many would consider civil offenses as disturbances to the "king's peace." As Colson and Van Ness (1989, p. 46) state: "Anyone who committed a crime violated this peace, thus violating the king. The king insisted that such cases be brought to his courts, which effectively gave him control over all criminal cases. . . . The king had not only taken the place of victims before the law; he had also taken away their right to be repaid for their losses." While the problems of the former legal systems were legion, the new system focused on the offenders rather than the victims. Instead of victims being the center of the resolution of the situation, the chief issues in "processing the case" focused on what to do with the offender.

3. This is not to say that fear of crime cannot be irrational. It can. Yet to demonstrate irrationality, one would need to show very low risk for a community and an individual who pretty much "lives in" that community. Even then, the specter of "drive-by shootings" in America defy the concept of little or no risk. The point is that most American's judgments of risk correlate with objective risk, and other studies have shown that people are fairly accurate in their estimates of crime (e.g., Warr 1980).

It appears there are two basic ways of defining excessive or irrational fear. First, using a statistical model, some people may experience fear which is higher than the norm (e.g., more than one standard deviation above the mean). One could define that as irrational but by doing so, one should also control for all the ecological, lifestyle, and personal characteristics. Still, there would be no objective standard for fear. Some people would always be classified as manifesting exaggerated fear. The other way to attempt to establish irrational fear would be to clinically identify some type of psychiatric disorder or irrationality in other life domains. Again, "irrational" fear of crime is possible but the results of the present investigation suggest that it is fairly rare. People's fear of crime correlates well with perceived risk and other variables in the risk interpretation model.

4. One of the limitations of trying to link official crime risk with fear of crime concerns the units of analysis. Crime rates are compiled by the Federal Bureau of Investigation for all counties and selected cities and small towns. The county is probably a good unit of measurement when making comparisons across the nation. Since there is ample variation across the United States, or even in one state, county crime rates provide a meaningful unit of analysis (Miethe and Lee 1984). Still, some counties

are large units and show considerable variation within their boundaries. One of the limitations of the present study is that it uses only county rates of crime. While the present study used neighborhood characteristics such as incivility and cohesion to probe the respondent's local environment, we need research linking ecological characteristics using various units of analysis. Research using various units of analysis will enable rigorous tests of the possibility of ecological and cultural influences on perceived risk and fear of crime. If different units of analysis yield similar findings, then the robustness of the findings is clearly established.

REFERENCES

Akers, Ronald L., Anthony J. LaGreca, Christine Sellers and John Cochrane. 1987. "Fear of Crime and Victimization Among the Elderly in Different Types of Communities." *Criminology* 25:487–505.

Aldrich, John H. and Forrest D. Nelson. 1984. *Linear Probability, Logit, and Probit Models.* Newbury Park, California: Sage.

Alexander, J. C., B. Giesen, R. Munch and N. J. Smelser. 1987. *The Micro-Macro Link.* Berkeley: University of California Press.

American Veterinary Medical Association. 1983. *The Veterinary Services Market. Volumes I and II.* Overland Park, KS: Charles, Charles, and Associates.

Associated Press. 1993. "Women Aiming at Staying Safe." *Journal and Courier* (Gannett News Service). Lafayette, IN: February 7.

Bachman, Ronet. 1992. *Elderly Victims.* Washington, DC: U.S. Department of Justice, Bureau of Justice Statistics.

Baker, Mary H., Barbara C. Nienstedt, Ronald S. Everett and Richard McCleary. 1983. "Impact of a Crime Wave: Perceptions, Fear and Confidence in the Police." *Law and Society Review* 17:319–335.

Balkin, Steve. 1979. "Victimization Rates, Safety, and Fear of Crime." *Social Problems* 26:343–358.

Bankston, William B. and Carol Y. Thompson. 1989. "Carrying Firearms for Protection: A Causal Model." *Sociological Inquiry* 59:75–87.

Bankston, William B., Carol Y. Thompson, Quentin A. L. Jenkins and Craig J. Forsyth. 1990. "The Influence of Fear of Crime, Gender, and Southern Culture on Carrying Firearms for Protection." *Sociological Quarterly* 31:287–305.

Baron, Larry and Murray A. Straus. 1989. *Four Theories of Rape in American Society.* New Haven: Yale University Press.

Baumer, Terry L. 1978. "Research on Fear of Crime in the United States." *Victimology* 3:254–264.

Baumer, Terry L. 1985. "Testing a General Model of Fear of Crime: Data from a National Sample." *Journal of Research in Crime and Delinquency* 22:239–255.

Beasley, Ronald W. and George Antunes. 1974. "The Etiology of Urban Crime: An Ecological Analysis." *Criminology* 11:439–461.

Becker, Marshall H. and Irwin M. Rosenstock. 1989. "Health Promotion, Disease Prevention, and Program Retention." Pp. 284–305 in *Handbook of Medical Sociology*, 4th ed., edited by Howard E. Freeman and Sol Levine. New Jersey: Prentice Hall.

Berger, Peter L. 1963. *Invitation to Sociology: A Humanistic Perspective.* Garden City, NJ: Anchor.

Binstock, Robert H. 1983. "The Aged as Scapegoat." *The Gerontologist* 23:136–143.

Blumer, Herbert. 1969. *Symbolic Interactionism: Perspective and Method.* Englewood Cliffs, NJ: Prentice Hall.

Blumer, Herbert. 1979. *Critiques of Research in the Social Sciences: An Appraisal of Thomas and Znaniecki's The Polish Peasant in Europe and America.* New Brunswick, NJ: Transaction.

Bollen, Kenneth A. 1989. *Structural Equations with Latent Variables.* New York: John Wiley.

Bourque, Linda Brookover. 1989. *Defining Rape.* Durham, NC: Duke University Press.

Box, Steven, Chris Hale and Glen Andrews. 1988. "Explaining Fear of Crime." *British Journal of Criminology* 28:340–356.

Brantingham, Paul, Patricia Brantingham and Diane Butcher. 1986. "Perceived and Actual Crime Risks." Pp. 139–159 in *Metropolitan Crime Patterns*, edited by Robert Figleo, Simon Hakim and George Rengert. New York: Willow Tree Press.

Braungart, Margaret M., Richard G. Braungart and William J. Hoyer. 1980. "Age, Sex, and Social Factors in Fear of Crime." *Sociological Focus* 13:55–56.

Braungart, Margaret M., William J. Hoyer and Richard G. Braungart. 1979. "Fear of Crime and the Elderly." In Arnold P. Goldstein, William J. Hoyer and Phillip J. Monti (Eds.), *Police and the Elderly.* New York: Pergamon Press.

Brillon, Yves. 1987. *Victimization and Fear of Crime Among the Elderly.* Toronto: Butterworths.

Bureau of Justice Statistics. 1989. *Households Touched By Crime, 1988.* Washington, DC: U.S. Department of Justice, Office of Justice Programs.

Bureau of Justice Statistics. 1991. *Criminal Victimization 1990.* Washington, DC: U.S. Department of Justice, Office of Justice Programs.

Bursik, Robert J., Jr. and Harold G. Grasmick, Jr. 1993. *Neighborhoods and Crime: The Dimensions of Effective Community Control.* New York: Lexington Books.

Bursik, Robert J., Jr. and Jim Webb. 1982. "Community Change and Patterns of Delinquency." *American Journal of Sociology* 88:24–42.

Burt, Ronald S. 1976. "Interpretational Confounding of Unobserved Variables in Structural Equation Models." *Sociological Methods and Research* 5:3–52.

Chadwick-Jones, J. K. 1976. *Social Exchange Theory: Its Structure and Influence in Social Psychology.* New York: Academic Press.

Charon, Joel M. 1989. *Symbolic Interactionism,* 3d ed. Prentice-Hall.

Clarke, Alan H. and Margaret Lewis. 1982. "Fear of Crime Among the Elderly." *British Journal of Criminology* 22:49–62.

Cleary, Paul D. and Ronald Angel. 1984. "The Analysis of Relationships Involving Dichotomous Dependent Variables." *Journal of Health and Social Behavior* 25:334–348.

Clemente, Frank and Michael Kleiman. 1976. "Fear of Crime Among the Aged." *Gerontologist* 16:207–210.

Clemente, Frank and Michael Kleiman. 1977. "Fear of Crime in the United States: A Multivariate Analysis." *Social Forces* 56:519–531.

Cohen, Jacob and Patricia Cohen. 1975. *Applied Multiple Regression/ Correlation Analysis for the Behavioral Sciences.* Hillsdale, NJ: Lawrence Erlbaum Associates.

Cohen, Lawrence E. and Marcus Felson. 1979. "Social Change and Crime Rate Trends: A Routine Activity Approach." *American Sociological Review* 44:588–608.

Cohen, Lawrence E., Marcus Felson and Kenneth C. Land. 1980. "Property Crime Rates in the United States: A Macrodynamic Analysis, 1947–1977; with Ex Ante Forecasts for the Mid-1980s." *American Journal of Sociology* 86:90–118.

Cohrssen, John J. and Vincent T. Covello. 1989. *Risk Analysis: A Guide to Principles and Methods for Analyzing Health and Environmental Risks.* Washington, DC: Council on Environmental Quality, Executive Office of the President.

Coleman, James S. 1990. *Foundations of Social Theory.* Cambridge, MA: Belknap Press.

Colson, Charles. 1993. "Making Sense of Senseless Crime." *Jubilee* (November), p. 7.

Colson, Charles and Daniel Van Ness. 1989. *Convicted: New Hope for Ending America's Crime Crisis.* Westchester, IL: Crossway.

Conklin, John E. 1975. *The Impact of Crime.* New York: MacMillan.

Cook, Fay Lomax and Thomas D. Cook. 1976. "Evaluating the Rhetoric of Crisis: A Case Study of Criminal Victimization of the Elderly." *Social Service Review* 50:632–646.

Covington, Jeanette and Ralph B. Taylor. 1991. "Fear of Crime in Urban Residential Neighborhoods: Implications of Between- and Within-Neighborhood Sources for Current Models." *Sociological Quarterly* 32:231–249.

Crutchfield, Robert, Michael Geerken and Walter R. Gove. 1983. "Crime Rates and Social Integration." *Criminology* 20:467–478.

Cutler, Stephen J. 1980. "Safety on the Streets: Cohort Changes in Fear." *International Journal of Aging and Human Development* 10:373–384.

Dean, Charles W. and Mary deBruyn-Kops. 1982. *The Crime and Consequences of Rape*. Springfield, IL: Charles C. Thomas.

DeFronzo, James. 1979. "Fear of Crime and Handgun Ownership." *Criminology* 17:331–339.

Deutscher, Irwin. 1973. *What We Say/What We Do: Sentiments and Acts*. Glenview, IL: Scott, Foresman.

Douglas, Mary. 1985. *Risk Acceptability According to the Social Sciences*. New York: Russell Sage Foundation.

DuBow, Fredric, Edward McCabe and Gail Kaplan. 1979. *Reactions to Crime: A Critical Review of the Literature*. Washington, D.C.: National Institute of Law Enforcement and Criminal Justice; U.S. Government Printing Office.

Durkheim, Emile. 1895, 1933. *The Division of Labor in Society*. Translated by George Simpson. Glencoe, IL: The Free Press.

Erikson, Kai. 1966. *Wayward Puritans*. New York: Wiley.

Fattah, E. A. and V. F. Sacco. 1989. *Crime and Victimization of the Elderly*. New York: Springer-Verlag.

Federal Bureau of Investigation. 1990 (and previous years: 1960–1989). *Uniform Crime Reports for the United States (Crime in the United States)*. Washington, DC: U.S. Government Printing Office.

Ferraro, Kenneth F. 1992. "Self and Older-People Referents in Evaluating Life Problems." *Journal of Gerontology: Social Sciences* 47:S105–114.

Ferraro, Kenneth F. and Randy LaGrange. 1987. "The Measurement of Fear of Crime." *Sociological Inquiry* 57:70–101.

Ferraro, Kenneth F. and Randy L. LaGrange. 1988. "Are Older People Afraid of Crime?" *Journal of Aging Studies* 2:277–287.

Ferraro, Kenneth F. and Randy L. LaGrange. 1992. "Are Older People Most Afraid of Crime? Reconsidering Age Differences in Fear of Victimization." *Journal of Gerontology: Social Sciences* 47:S233–244.

Ferraro, Kenneth F., Randy L. LaGrange and William C. McCready. 1990. *Are Older People Afraid of Crime? Examining Risk, Fear, and Constrained Behavior*. Final report to the AARP Andrus Foundation. DeKalb: Northern Illinois University.

Fischhoff, Baruch, Ann Bostrom and Marilyn Jacobs Quadrel. 1993. "Risk Perception and Communication." *Annual Review of Public Health* 14:183–203.

Frey, James H. 1983. *Survey Research by Telephone*. Beverly Hills, CA: Sage.

Furstenberg, Frank F., Jr. 1971. "Public Reaction to Crime in the Streets." *American Scholar* 40:601–610.

Garofalo, James. 1979. "Victimization and the Fear of Crime." *Journal of Research in Crime and Delinquency* 16:80–97.

Garofalo, James. 1981. "The Fear of Crime: Causes and Consequences." *Journal of Criminal Law and Criminology* 72:839–857.

Garofalo, James and John Laub. 1978. "The Fear of Crime: Broadening Our Perspective." *Victimology* 3:242–253.

Giles-Sims, Jean. 1984. "A Multivariate Analysis of Perceived Likelihood of Victimization and Degree of Worry About Crime Among Older People." *Victimology* 9:222–233.

Goffman, Erving. 1971. *Relations in Public.* New York: Harper Colophon Books.

Gomme, Ian M. 1986. "Fear of Crime Among Canadians: A Multi-Variate Analysis." *Journal of Criminal Justice* 14:249–258.

Gordon, Margaret T. and Stephanie Riger. 1989. *The Female Fear.* New York: Free Press.

Gould, Peter F. and R. White. 1974. *Mental Maps.* Baltimore: Penguin.

Gove, Walter R., Michael Hughes and Michael Geerken. 1985. "Are Uniform Crime Reports a Valid Indicator of the Index Crime? An Affirmative Answer with Minor Qualifications." *Criminology* 23:451–501.

Hall, Edward T. 1966. *The Hidden Dimension.* Garden City, NY: Anchor.

Harlow, Caroline Wolf. 1991. *Female Victims of Violent Crime.* Washington, DC: U.S. Department of Justice, Bureau of Justice Statistics.

Harris, Keith D. 1976. "Cities and Crime: A Geographic Model." *Criminology* 14:369–386.

Hartnagel, Timothy F. 1979. "The Perception of Fear of Crime: Implications for Neighborhood Cohesion, Social Activity, and Community Affect." *Social Forces* 58:176–193.

Hawley, Amos. 1950. *Human Ecology: A Theory of Community Structure.* New York: Ronald.

Hayduk, Leslie A. 1987. *Structural Equation Modeling with LISREL.* Baltimore: Johns Hopkins University Press.

Hedley, R. Alan. 1986. "Everybody But Me: Self-Other Referents in Social Research." *Sociological Inquiry* 56:245–258.

Heise, David R. 1975. *Causal Analysis.* New York: John Wiley.

Henig, J. and M. G. Maxfield. 1978. "Reducing Fear of Crime: Strategies for Intervention." *Victimology* 3:297–313.

Hindelang, Michael J., Michael R. Gottfredson and James Garofalo. 1978. *Victims of Personal Crime: An Empirical Foundation for a Theory of Personal Victimization.* Cambridge, MA: Ballinger.

Hunter, Albert. 1978. "Symbols of Incivility: Social Disorder and Fear of Crime in Urban Neighborhoods." Paper presented at the Annual

Meeting of the American Society of Criminology, Dallas, TX, November.

Jaehnig, Walter B., David H. Weaver and Fredrick Fico. 1981. "Reporting Crime and Fear of Crime in Three Communities." *Journal of Communication* 31:88–96.

Janson, Philip and Louis K. Ryder. 1983. "Crime and the Elderly: The Relationship Between Risk and Fear." *The Gerontologist* 23:207–212.

Jaycox, Victoria. 1978. "The Elderly's Fear of Crime: Rational or Irrational." *Victimology* 3:329–334.

Jeffords, Clifford, R. 1983. "The Situational Relationship Between Age and Fear of Crime." *International Journal of Aging and Human Development* 17:103–111.

Joreskog, Karl G. and Dag Sorbom. 1988. *LISREL 7: A Guide to the Program and Applications*. Chicago: SPSS Inc.

Journal and Courier. 1994. "Violence Down, Gun Deaths Up." (Gannett News Service), Lafayette, IN: February 27, p. A3.

Kahneman, Daniel, Paul Slovic and Amos Tversky (editors). 1982. *Judgment Under Uncertainty: Heuristics and Biases*. Cambridge: Cambridge University Press.

Kanin, Eugene J. 1985. "Date Rapists: Differential Sexual Socialization and Relative Deprivation." *Archives of Sexual Behavior* 14:219–231.

Karmen, Andrew A. 1991. "Victims of Crime," in *Criminology: A Contemporary Handbook*, edited by Joseph F. Sheley, 121–138. Belmont, CA: Wadsworth.

Kennedy, Edward. 1972. *Hearings Before the Subcommittee on Housing for the Elderly*, 92d Cong., 2d sess. Washington, DC: U.S. Congress, Senate, Special Committee on Aging.

Kennedy, Leslie W. and Harvey Krahn. 1984. "Rural-urban Origin and Fear of Crime: The Case for 'Rural Baggage.'" *Rural Sociology* 49:247–260.

Kennedy, Leslie W. and Robert A. Silverman. 1985. "Significant Others and Fear of Crime Among the Elderly." *International Journal of Aging and Human Development* 20:241–256.

Kerlinger, Fred N. 1986. *Foundations of Behavioral Research* (third edition). New York: Holt, Rinehart and Winston.

Kim, Jae-On and Charles W. Mueller. 1978. *Factor Analysis: Statistical Methods and Practical Issues*. Newbury Park, CA: Sage.

Kleinman, Paula H. and Deborah S. David. 1973. "Victimization and Perception of Crime in a Ghetto Community." *Criminology* 11:307–339.

LaGory, Mark and John Pipkin. 1981. *Urban Social Space*. Belmont, CA: Wadsworth.

LaGrange, Randy L. and Kenneth F. Ferraro. 1987. "The Elderly's Fear of Crime: A Critical Examination of the Research." *Research on Aging* 9:372–391.

LaGrange, Randy L. and Kenneth F. Ferraro. 1989. "Assessing Age and Gender Differences in Perceived Risk and Fear of Crime." *Criminology* 27:697–719.

LaGrange, Randy L., Kenneth F. Ferraro and Michael Supancic. 1992. "Perceived Risk and Fear of Crime: Role of Social and Physical Incivilities." *Journal of Research in Crime and Delinquency* 29:311–334.

Langlie, Jean K. 1977. "Social Networks, Health Beliefs, and Preventive Health Behavior." *Journal of Health and Social Behavior* 18:244–260.

Lawton, M. Powell and Sylvia Yaffe. 1980. "Victimization and Fear of Crime in Elderly Public Housing Tenants." *Journal of Gerontology* 35:768–779.

Lebowitz, Barry. 1975. "Age and Fearfulness: Personal and Situational Factors." *Journal of Gerontology* 30:696–700.

Lee, Gary R. 1982a. "Residential Location and Fear of Crime Among the Elderly." *Rural Sociology* 47:655–669.

Lee, Gary R. 1982b. "Sex Differences in Fear of Crime Among Older People." *Research on Aging* 4:284–298.

Lee, Gary R. 1983. "Social Integration and Fear of Crime." *Journal of Gerontology* 38:745–750.

Lewis, Dan A. and Michael G. Maxfield. 1980. "Fear in the Neighborhoods: An Investigation of the Impact of Crime." *Journal of Research in Crime and Delinquency* 17:160–189.

Lewis, Dan A. and Greta Salem. 1986. *Fear of Crime: Incivility and the Production of a Social Problem*. New Brunswick, NJ: Transaction.

Liang, Jersey and Mary C. Sengstock. 1981. "The Risk of Personal Victimization Among the Aged." *Journal of Gerontology* 36:463–471.

Lindquist, John H. and Janice M. Duke. 1982. "The Elderly Victim at Risk: Explaining the Fear-Victimization Paradox." *Criminology* 20:115–126.

Liska, Allen E. and William Baccaglini. 1990. "Feeling Safe By Comparison: Crime in the Newspapers." *Social Problems* 37:360–374.

Liska, Allen E., Joseph Lawrence and Andrew Sanchirico. 1982. "Fear of Crime as a Social Fact." *Social Forces* 60:760–770.

Liska, Allen E., Andrew Sanchirico and Mark D. Reed. 1988. "Fear of Crime and Constrained Behavior: Specifying and Estimating a Reciprocal Effects Model." *Social Forces* 66:827–837.

Liska, Allen E. and Barbara D. Warner. 1991. "Functions of Crime: A Paradoxical Process." *American Journal of Sociology* 96:1441–1463.

Longino, Helen E. 1980. "Pornography, Oppression, and Freedom: A Closer Look" in *Take Back the Night: Women on Pornography*, edited by Laura Lederer, 40–54. New York: William Morrow.

Maguire, Kathleen and Timothy J. Flanagan. 1991. *Sourcebook of Criminal Justice Statistics 1990*. Washington, DC: U.S. Department of Justice, Bureau of Justice Statistics (U.S. Government Printing Office).

Maxfield, Michael G. 1984. "The Limits of Vulnerability in Explaining Fear of Crime: A Comparative Neighborhood Analysis." *Journal of Research in Crime and Delinquency* 21:233–250.

McPherson, Marlys. 1978. "Realities and Perceptions of Crime at the Neighborhood Level." *Victimology* 3:319–328.

Mead, George H. 1934. *Mind, Self, and Society*. Chicago: University of Chicago Press.

Melbin, Murray. 1978. "Night as Frontier." *American Sociological Review* 43:3–22.

Miethe, Terance D. and Gary R. Lee. 1984. "Fear of Crime Among Older People: A Reassessment of the Predictive Power of Crime-Related Factors." *Sociological Quarterly* 25:397–415.

Moeller, Gertrude L. 1989. "Fear of Criminal Victimization: The Effect of Neighborhood Racial Composition." *Sociological Inquiry* 59:208–221.

Mullen, Robert E. and Joseph F. Donnermeyer. 1985. "Age, Trust, and Perceived Safety from Crime in Rural Areas." *The Gerontologist* 25:237–242.

National Institute of Justice. 1992. *Research and Evaluation Plan*. Washington, D.C.: U.S. Department of Justice.

Nettler, Gwynn. 1974. *Explaining Crime*. New York: McGraw-Hill.

Norton, Lee and Michael Courlander. 1982. "Fear of Crime Among the Elderly: The Role of Crime Prevention Programs." *The Gerontologist* 22:388–393.

Ollenburger, Jane C. 1981. "Criminal Victimization and Fear of Crime." *Research on Aging* 3:101–118.

Ortega, Suzanne L. and Jessie L. Myles. 1987. "Race and Gender Effects on the Fear of Crime: An Interactive Model with Age." *Criminology* 25:133–152.

Park, Robert E. and Ernest W. Burgess. 1925 [1967]. *The City*. Chicago: University of Chicago Press.

Parker, Keith D. 1988. "Black-White Differences in Perceptions of Fear of Crime." *Journal of Social Psychology* 128:487–494.

Parker, Keith D. and Melvin C. Ray. 1990. "Fear of Crime: An Assessment of Related Factors." *Sociological Spectrum* 10:29–40.

Parks, M. Jean. 1990. "Rape Victims' Perceptions of Long-Term Effects Three or More Years Post Rape." Pp. 21–37 in *The Victimology*

Handbook: Research Findings, Treatment, and Public Policy, edited by Emilio C. Viano. New York: Garland Publishing.

Podolefsky, Aaron and Frederic DuBow. 1981. *Strategies for Community Crime Prevention: Collective Responses to Crime in Urban America.* Springfield, IL: Charles C. Thomas Publisher.

Pollack, Lance and Arthur H. Patterson. 1980. "Territoriality and Fear of Crime in Elderly and Nonelderly Homeowners." *Journal of Social Psychology* 111:119–129.

Pyle, Gerald F. 1990. "Systematic Sociospatial Variation in Perceptions of Crime Location and Severity." Pp. 219–45 in *Crime: A Spatial Perspective* edited by Daniel E. Georges-Abeyie and Keith D. Harries. New York: Columbia University Press.

Pyle, Gerald F. and Edward W. Hanten, et al. 1974. *The Spatial Dynamics of Crime.* Chicago: University of Chicago Department of Geography, Research Paper 159.

Riger, Stephanie and Margaret T. Gordon. 1981. "The Fear of Rape: A Study in Social Control." *Journal of Social Issues* 37:71–92.

Riger, Stephanie, Margaret T. Gordon and Robert Le Bailly. 1978. "Women's Fear of Crime: From Blaming to Restricting the Victim." *Victimology* 3:274–284.

Quinney, Richard. 1970. *The Social Reality of Crime.* Boston: Little, Brown.

Sacco, Vincent F. 1990. "Gender, Fear, and Victimization: A Preliminary Application of Power-Control Theory." *Sociological Spectrum* 10:485–506.

Sarbin, Theodore R. and Norman L. Farberow. 1952. "Contributions to Role-Taking Theory: A Clinical Study of Self and Role." *Journal of Abnormal and Social Psychology* 47:117–125.

Sarnoff, Irving and Phillip G. Zimbardo. 1961. "Anxiety, Fear, and Social Affiliation." *Journal of Abnormal Social Psychology* 62:356–363.

Schram, Donna D. 1978. "Rape." Pp. 53–79 in *The Victimization of Women,* edited by Jane Roberts Chapman and Margaret Gates. Beverly Hills, CA: Sage.

Schuman, Howard and Stanley Presser. 1981. *Questions and Answers in Attitude Surveys: Experiments on Question Form, Wording and Context.* New York: Academic Press.

Schwarzenegger, Christian. 1991. "Public Attitudes to Crime: Findings of the Zurich Victim Survey." Pp. 681–730 in *Victimological Research: Stocktaking and Prospects* (volume 50 of *Victims and Criminal Justice*), edited by G. Kaiser, H. Kury and H.-J. Albrecht. Freiburg i.Br.: Max-Planck-Institute.

Schwarzenegger, Christian. 1992. *Die Einstellungen der Bevolkerung zur Kriminalitat und Verbrechenskontrolle (Public Attitudes to Crime and Crime Control)*. Freiburg i.Br.: Max-Planck-Institute.

Selye, Hans. 1956. *The Stress of Life*. New York: McGraw-Hill.

Selye, Hans. 1974. *Stress Without Distress*. Philadelphia: J. B. Lippincott.

Silberman, Charles. 1981. "Fear." Pp. 5–21 in *Under Law: Readings in Criminal Justice*, edited by Robert C. Culbertson and Mark T. Tezak. Prospect Heights, Ill.: Waveland Press, Inc.

Singelmann, Peter. 1972. "Exchange As Symbolic Interaction: Convergence Between Two Theoretical Perspectives." *American Sociological Review* 37:414–423.

Skogan, Wesley G. 1987. "The Impact of Victimization on Fear." *Crime and Delinquency* 33:135–154.

Skogan, Wesley G. 1990. *Disorder and Decline: Crime and the Spiral of Decay in American Neighborhoods*. New York: Free Press.

Skogan, Wesley G. and Michael G. Maxfield. 1981. *Coping with Crime*. Beverly Hills, CA: Sage.

Slovic, Paul, Baruch Fischhoff and Sarah Lichtenstein. 1982. "Facts Versus Fears: Understanding Perceived Risk." Pp. 463–489 in *Judgment Under Uncertainty: Heuristics and Biases*, edited by Daniel Kahneman, Paul Slovic and Amos Tversky. Cambridge: Cambridge University Press.

Smith, Christopher J. and Gene E. Patterson. 1990. "Cognitive Mapping and the Subjective Geography of Crime." Pp. 203–18 in *Crime: A Spatial Perspective*, edited by Daniel E. Georges-Abeyie and Keith D. Harries. New York: Columbia University Press.

Smith, Lynn Newhart and Gary D. Hill. 1991. "Perceptions of Crime Seriousness and Fear of Crime." *Sociological Focus* 24:315–327.

Smith, Michael D. 1988. "Women's Fear of Violent Crime: An Exploratory Test of a Feminist Hypothesis." *Journal of Family Violence* 3:29–38.

Stafford, Mark C. and Omer R. Galle. 1984. "Victimization Rates, Exposure to Risk, and Fear of Crime." *Criminology* 22:173–185.

Stagner, Ross. 1981. "Stress, Strain, Coping, and Defense." *Research on Aging*, 3:3–32.

Stahura, John M. and Richard C. Hollinger. 1988. "A Routine Activities Approach to Suburban Arson Rates." *Sociological Spectrum* 8:349–369.

Stahura, John M. and John J. Sloan III. 1988. "Urban Stratification of Places, Routine Activities and Suburban Crime Rates." *Social Forces* 66:1102–1118.

Stark, Rodney. 1992. *Sociology* (4th edition). Belmont, CA: Wadsworth.

Stebbins, Robert A. 1967. "A Theory of the Definition of the Situation." *Canadian Review of Sociology and Anthropology* 4:148–64.

Stebbins, Robert A. 1969. "Studying the Definition of the Situation: Theory and Field Research Strategies." *Canadian Review of Sociology and Anthropology* 6:193–211.

Stinchcombe, Arthur L., Rebecca Adams, Carol A. Heimer, Kim Lane Scheppele, Tom W. Smith and D. Garth Taylor. 1980. *Crime and Punishment: Changing Attitudes in America*. San Francisco: Jossey-Bass.

Stryker, Sheldon. 1980. *Symbolic Interactionism: A Social Structural Version*. Menlo Park, CA: Benjamin/Cummings.

Sundeen, Richard A. and James T. Mathieu. 1976. "The Fear of Crime and Its Consequences Among Elderly in Three Urban Communities." *The Gerontologist* 16:211–219.

Swafford, Michael. 1980. "Three Parametric Techniques for Contingency Table Analysis: A Nontechnical Commentary." *American Sociological Review* 45:664–690.

Taub, Richard P., D. Garth Taylor and Jan D. Dunham. 1984. *Paths of Neighborhood Change: Race and Crime in Urban America*. Chicago: University of Chicago Press.

Taylor, D. Garth, Richard P. Taub and Bruce Peterson. 1986. "Crime, Community Organization, and Causes of Neighborhood Decline." Pp. 161–77 in *Metropolitan Crime Patterns*, edited by Robert Figleo, Simon Hakim and George Rengert. New York: Willow Tree Press.

Taylor, Ralph B. and Margaret Hale. 1986. "Testing Alternative Models of Fear of Crime." *Journal of Criminal Law and Criminology* 77:151–189.

Taylor, Ralph B., Stephen D. Gottfredson and Sidney Brower. 1980. "The Defensibility of Defensible Space: A Critical Review and a Synthetic Framework for Future Research." Pp. 53–71 in *Understanding Crime: Current Theory and Research*, edited by Travis Hirschi and Michael Gottredson. Beverly Hills: Sage Publications.

Taylor, Ralph B., Stephen D. Gottfredson and Sidney Brower. 1984. "Block Crime and Fear: Defensible Space, Local Social Ties, and Territorial Functioning." *Journal of Research in Crime and Delinquency* 21:303–331.

Thomas, Charles W. and Jeffrey M. Hyman. 1977. "Perceptions of Crime, Fear of Victimization, and Public Perceptions of Police Performance." *Journal of Police Science and Administration.* 5:305–317.

Thomas, Piri. 1967. *Down These Mean Streets*. New York: Alfred A. Knopf.

Thomas, William I. 1923. *The Unadjusted Girl*. Boston: Little, Brown.

Thomas, William I. and Dorothy Swaine Thomas. 1928. *The Child in America*. New York: Knopf.

Thomas, William I. and Florian Znaniecki. (1918) 1974. *The Polish Peasant in Europe and America.* New York: Octagon.

Time. 1976. "The Elderly: Prisoners of Fear." 108:21 (Nov. 29).

Time. 1985. "Up in Arms Over Crime." 125:28–34 (April 8).

Toennies, Ferdinand. 1963 [1887]. *Community and Society (Gemeinschaft and Gesellschaft).* New York: Harper and Row.

Tversky, Amos and Daniel Kahneman. 1982. "Causal Schemas in Judgments Under Uncertainty." Pp. 117–128 in *Judgment Under Uncertainty: Heuristics and Biases,* edited by Daniel Kahneman, Paul Slovic and Amos Tversky. Cambridge: Cambridge University Press.

Tyler, Tom R. 1980. "Impact of Directly and Indirectly Experienced Events: The Origin of Crime-Related Judgments and Behaviors." *Journal of Personality and Social Psychology* 39:13–28.

Tyler, Tom R. and Fay Lomax Cook. 1984. "The Mass Media and Judgments of Risk: Distinguishing Impact on Personal and Societal Level Judgments." *Journal of Personality and Social Psychology* 47:693–708.

U.S. Attorney General's Commission on Pornography. 1986. *Final Report of the Attorney General's Commission on Pornography.* Washington, DC: U.S. Department of Justice, Government Printing Office.

U.S. Bureau of the Census. 1989. *Statistical Abstract of the United States: 1989.* Washington, DC: U.S. Government Printing Office.

U.S. Department of Justice. 1977. *San Diego: Public Attitudes about Crime, National Crime Survey Report.* No. SD-NCS-C-30, NJC-42245. Washington, DC: U.S. Government Printing Office.

Volkhart, Edmund H. (ed.) 1951. *Social Behavior and Personality: Contributions of W. I. Thomas to Theory and Research.* New York: Social Science Research Council.

Waller, Irvin and Norman Okihiro. 1978. *Burglary: The Victims and the Public.* Toronto: University of Toronto Press.

Ward, Russell A., Mark LaGory and Susan R. Sherman. 1986. "Fear of Crime Among the Elderly As Person/Environment Interaction." *Sociological Quarterly* 27:327–341.

Warr, Mark. 1980. "The Accuracy of Public Beliefs About Crime." *Social Forces* 59:456–470.

Warr, Mark. 1982. "The Accuracy of Public Beliefs About Crime: Further Evidence." *Criminology* 20:185–204.

Warr, Mark. 1984. "Fear of Victimization: Why Are Women and the Elderly More Afraid?" *Social Science Quarterly* 65:681–702.

Warr, Mark. 1985. "Fear of Rape Among Urban Women." *Social Problems* 32:238–250.

Warr, Mark. 1990. "Dangerous Situations: Social Context and Fear of Victimization." *Social Forces* 68:891–907.

Warr, Mark and Mark Stafford. 1983. "Fear of Victimization: A Look at the Proximate Causes." *Social Forces* 61:1033–1043.

Wheaton, Blair, Bengt Muthen, Duane F. Alwin and Gene F. Summers. 1977. "Assessing Reliability and Stability in Panel Models." Pp. 84–136 in *Sociological Methodology*, edited by David R. Heise. San Francisco: Jossey-Bass.

Williams, Robin M., Jr. 1970. *American Society: A Sociological Interpretation*. New York: Alfred A. Knopf.

Wilson, James Q. 1968. "The Urban Unease: Community vs. City." *The Public Interest* 12:25–39.

Wilson, James Q. 1983. *Thinking About Crime*, rev. ed. New York: Basic Books.

Wilson, James Q. 1993. *The Moral Sense*. New York: Free Press.

Wilson, James Q. and George L. Kelling. 1982. "Broken Windows." *Atlantic Monthly* 249:29–38.

Wilson, James Q. and George L. Kelling. 1985. "Broken Windows: The Police and Neighborhood Safety." Pp. 220–28 in *The Ambivalent Force*, edited by A. Blumberg and E. Niederhoffer. New York: Holt, Rinehart, and Winston.

Wirtz, Philip W. and Adele V. Harrell. 1987. "The Effects of Threatening Versus Nonthreatening Previous Life Events on Levels of Fear in Rape Victims." *Violence and Victims* 2:89–98.

Wright, James D. 1991. "Guns and Crime," in *Criminology: A Contemporary Handbook*, edited by Joseph F. Sheley, 441–477. Belmont, CA: Wadsworth.

Yin, Peter. 1980. "Fear of Crime Among the Elderly: Some Issues and Suggestions." *Social Problems* 27:492–504.

Yin, Peter. 1982. "Fear of Crime as a Problem for the Elderly." *Social Problems* 30:240–245.

Yin, Peter. 1988. *Victimization and the Aged*. Springfield, IL: Charles C. Thomas.

NAME INDEX

SUBJECT INDEX